Dr David Armstrong's

The Right Words
Teaching the Post-16 to Spell

www.trts.co.uk

Teaching R~~eading Th~~ing

First published in 2004 by TRTS PUBLISHING

Printed in Great Britain by
Antony Rowe, Chippenham, Wiltshire

ISBN   1-900283-09-3

TRTS Publishing,
PO Box 1349, Wrexham, Wales, U.K. LL14 4ZA
Telephone: 01978-840868
Facsimile: 01978-845715
Email: books@trts.co.uk
Website: www.trts.co.uk

The Author

Dr David Armstrong is a specialist educational adviser/dyslexia consultant for a major college in Manchester and has worked across HE and FE, with commercial training providers and in Adult Education.

CONTENTS

Section 1: INTRODUCTION

Section 2: GETTING STARTED

Section 3: GRAPHOPHONICS

CONTENTS

Section 4: OTHER STRATEGIES

Section 5: SOME SAMPLE SESSIONS

CONCLUSION

CURRICULUM INDEX

TRTS THE RIGHT WORDS

Section 1: INTRODUCTION

Why Improve Spelling?

Spelling is often an emotional issue for those post-16. They may have experienced years of frustration and often realise that not being able to spell the words they want to use in their writing has impeded their overall progress in education and training. Poor spelling may even have blocked their career prospects because *they* have excluded themselves from jobs and careers that require good literacy skills.

The British post-16 education system, in common with other western countries, places an extremely heavy emphasis upon written evidence for progress and achievement. What students write in their portfolio, in marked assignments and in exams usually determines whether they achieve the qualification and whether they progress into work or further study/training.

If a student is struggling to spell words they are probably not giving their full attention to what they are writing (the content) and how it is organised (presentation). Because we measure academic achievement in literary terms this means that they are not achieving their potential.

To make things even worse, not being able to spell with consistent accuracy often has an enormously corrosive effect upon confidence. Before meeting you they may have been told by parents, friends and teachers that they are 'no good at writing' or a 'poor speller' and internalised what was a thoughtless comment or (mistakenly) intended as a way of motivating them. Students with poor spelling often avoid writing altogether or do the minimum required and sometimes who can blame them for feeling this way?

A major goal of this book is to break this cycle of under-achievement by giving you and your students the tools and strategies to deal with poor spelling. As such, in a small, practical way, it offers strategies for those working in post-16 education to deal with the larger issue of inclusion.

To make *The Right Words* more concrete and realistic, reference is made to 'Tony' and 'Jill'; two case studies of learners with particular spelling weaknesses and strengths.

There are five overriding reasons for improving spelling:

* motivation in learning and in terms of career/work opportunities

* self-esteem

* oral and written vocabulary

* the quality of written expression

* the quantity of written expression

Learners with poor spelling are often less motivated educationally because past difficulty with spelling has corroded their self-esteem. Lack of confidence in spelling frequently feeds a lack of confidence in their abilities generally and a cycle of academic under-performance is often implicated. Tasks that involve writing can become a source of unease or frustration. Those with more severe problems can come to avoid them altogether. This, in turn, exacerbates existing difficulties: if we never write, then the skills required are underdeveloped or lost altogether. Not being able to write multisyllabic words and use a dictionary effectively can even, for some learners contribute towards restricting their oral vocabulary and to poor overall skills with 'words'.

The Right Words and its Content

The Right Words is organised into 5 sections followed by a Conclusion. This introduction is **Section 1**.

Section 2 sets out how and, more importantly, why learners' problems with spelling are identified. It then goes on to show how improvement in spelling is planned, monitored and reviewed using an *Individual Learning Plan* (referred to later as an ILP). This is essentially a document where students' goals are recorded and where their progress is recorded. A standard format for an ILP is provided at the end of Section 4. ILPs are increasingly central to teaching and learning in the post-16 arena. They are a key point on the Adult Basic Skills Agency's 10-point standards list for the 'Q' (Quality) mark and currently seen, on a wider basis, as a standard tool for raising the standard of adult literacy and numeracy.

Section 3 tackles the potentially mystifying subject of graphophonics (often shortened to 'phonics). Despite an impressive sounding name graphophonics simply refers to the ways in which the look and the sounds of letters (or letter formations) relate. Often poor spelling can be the result of a learner not having correctly internalised the way in which this happens within English or having done so only partially. As a focus for teaching, graphophonics is firmly entrenched in the National Curriculum within primary schools where it figures large in teaching children to initially read and write.

Working with learners post-16 is a different context from working with children and Section 3 attempts to take this into account with the advice given about teaching the topic. A note of caution is also introduced here: while graphophonics is very valuable it is important that it is not the only strategy used for improving spelling.

Section 4 outlines a menu of possible strategies for improving spelling, including the most important: the LOOK, COVER, WRITE, CHECK method. All outlined strategies are explained and evaluated. A key point is that they can be used together in any combination that works for the learner. Jill and Tony's ILPs are included at the end of **Section 4** so that the reader can relate their needs to specific strategies and strategy combinations. Reference to elements within the Curriculum, are also suggested on their plans. At the end of **Section 4** brief advice is given on what to do if progress is not being made or if nothing seems to be working for a student.

Section 5 offers four ready-made groups sessions. The majority of teaching advocated in this book and in the wider world is on a one-to-one (1:1) basis. This teaching format is very valuable and is usually central to literacy work post-16. It is, however, not the only way in which spelling can be improved and group sessions provide a welcome break from 1:1 work, for student and teacher. The sessions offered are not set in stone: they are guidelines and can be altered given students' needs or timetabling issues.

In the Conclusion suggestion is made as to the positive long-term benefits that flow from improving a student's spelling.

The Curriculum

I began this book with the intention of providing an accessible guide as to how to teach those over 16 to spell, making some reference to the Literacy Core Curriculum (hereafter referred to as *The Curriculum)*. Whilst writing *The Right Words* it became apparent that what I was actually writing was a guide to using *The Curriculum,* exemplified by looking at how to teach spelling as a topic. What follows in this section reflects this change of emphasis and consists of:

- brief examination of the wider educational background to basic skills and Skills For Life

- advice on some of the wider issues around setting up provision for those who wish to improve their literacy and numeracy

- an explanation of the 3-dimensional 'focus' model which underpins *The Curriculum* and also how to understand and use this key guide to the national standards

Those who are already experienced teachers in this area may wish to go directly to subsequent sections but even they may glean some useful insights from the next few pages.

Background: The Ever-Increasing Stature of Skills for Life

The *Literacy Core Curriculum* and the equivalent for numeracy, were published in 2001 by the Basic Skills Agency on behalf on the British Government. It forms part of the government's national strategy to reduce the number of adults (those 16+) 'who struggle with basic reading, writing, spelling and maths' (p.1 *The Curriculum*). Notice how spelling is explicitly mentioned in this strategy statement: this prominence reflects the important place that it has within *The Curriculum* and feeds through into the number of elements (referenced sub-parts) which deal with improving spelling. When a tutor tackles spelling, using the guidance from this book to help them, they can be confident of addressing a significant area within the Literacy Core Curriculum for Adults. As I shall explain later, almost all of the 'word focus' part of *The Curriculum* (one-third of the overall literacy component) is made up of elements that are covered in this book.

Since 2001/2002 the Basic Skills Agency has offered a mobile national programme of training days based around the new core curricula, imaginatively called 'core curriculum training'. Literacy and numeracy are covered as separate areas and the training addresses how to understand and use the published standards in each area. While demanding – the training taking several days for literacy - they are extremely worthwhile to attend.

A broader change and, also useful background knowledge for anybody who teaches literacy, has been that post-2001, what was previously called basic skills (always an unfortunate name) has been officially re-branded as 'Skills For Life'. This is an umbrella term and covers not only what was described as basic skills but also what was referred to as ESOL (English for Speakers of Other Languages). Whilst still emerging, a key part of the Skills For Life agenda is the re-connection of all the different groups of adults who all have problems with literacy and numeracy. These diverse groups have, previously, been sectioned off into basic skills, ESOL, and/or those with learning difficulties of whatever form.

On another front, whilst writing this book there have been periodic releases in the press citing extra money from the government, money specifically targeted at improving literacy and numeracy (140 million pounds was the last figure reported in the press in late Spring 2004).

Taken together the appearance of the Core Curriculum, the Skills For Life Agenda and extra money for basic skills/Skills For Life provision, all disclose a concerted effort by the state to ensure that post-compulsory teaching meets the needs of those adults with literacy or numeracy difficulties. All these elements add up to an attempt to ensure professionalism across the post- 16 sector and to set standards for all to meet.

Personal experience indicates that from now on, good overall inspection results by Ofsted/ALI(Adult Learning Inspectorate) will be increasingly dependent upon how effectively problems with literacy/numeracy are identified and tackled amongst those 16+. It is also very likely that over the next few years duty-of-care responsibilities will increasingly come into play when, at enrolment via literacy assessment, colleges/education and training providers of whatever form, identify a student's weaknesses in reading or writing. In practice this will mean a responsibility *by them* to meet these needs rather just than refer students to other local services, as is often an institution's policy, or as I have seen happen occasionally, after picking up a student's weaknesses at initial assessment, file the problem away without any meaningful attempt at tackling it.

In short, within post-16 education and training, addressing the Skills For Life agenda is unavoidable. In practice this means that providing for those with literacy and/or numeracy problems using *The Curriculum* will be inescapable. By 'problems' I also mean those whom are below level 2 (approximately GCSE) or who have specific weaknesses in elements of their literacy, such as spelling. Those institutions and organisations that genuinely embrace the increasing emphasis placed upon what was, until recently described as basic skills will be in an advantageous position. Strength in this area they will increasingly attract the money and reputation to allow them to provide high-quality education and training for all the courses they offer. To education or training providers there are other benefits too. For those students enrolled upon a vocational or 'main programme' course, poor support for literacy difficulties is a major reason why students have poor attendance, low confidence, low expectations whilst on the course and often an underlying cause for them leaving study. This is especially true on vocational courses such as childcare, motor-vehicle studies, construction and catering, partly because these courses tend to attract learners who (mistakenly) suppose they are non-academic, with minimal written work.

If, Where You Work, All of This is New
Offering effective, imaginative and manageable provision for learners who have problems with their literacy or numeracy is however not a small task, particularly for organisations or institutions that have not offered this before or not offered it in any quantity. Practical and logistical issues can often undermine wordy strategy. Establishing courses, staff teams/structures and resources is both exciting and often stressful. Here is some very general advice to those setting up such provision, it is necessarily general because

TRTS THE RIGHT WORDS

the contexts in which those 16 + are taught (prisons, community centres, colleges, work-based training) are so very different:

- Having a clear idea of the profile (age, educational background, level of ability) of your learners, plus a clear idea of their reasons for attending tuition, will help you tailor your tuition or training. For example, what are the needs of your potential students? What do you already know about this? What are the central reasons they will want to improve their literacy: To pass their course? For career progression? To improve on poor academic results at school? Keep this information in focus when planning.

- Look at other, similar, providers in this area: how do they organise their courses or programme of study? How qualified are their staff? What kind of a staffing structure do they use? What is their staff-to-student ratio? What qualifications/accreditation do they offer to students?

- Will you/staff be working closely with subject tutors in delivering *The Curriculum or* will literacy/numeracy tuition/classes be offered as a separate package, taught by specialist literacy/numeracy tutors? Or, (my preference) will it be a mixture, where subject staff work closely with literacy/numeracy tutors but there is space for small-group or 1:1 teaching on specific literacy topics by a literacy/numeracy tutor.

- Speak to the Basic Skills Agency (Tel: 020-7045-4017): ask for their advice and support, especially in the early/planning stages of provision. Are they offering Core Curriculum/any other training –if so can you/ your staff attend? The agency also offers a 'Q' (quality) mark to institutions, this is gained by meeting 10 criteria explained in a booklet form – can you meet these criteria?

- Look at the skills, knowledge and experience of those who are assigned to be the literacy/numeracy teachers: have they/you the experience of teaching in this area before? - it is essential that some staff have this experience. Are they/you qualified to teach literacy and/or numeracy? -an approved teacher qualification is needed, plus Level 3/Level 4 subject specialist qualification – contact DfES Publications for details, listed in 'Resources required' at the end of this section). If they/you do not already have these qualifications then how long will it take them to get them? What is the overall timescale for setting up literacy and numeracy provision?

Two Common Contexts of Study

There are two common contexts in which literacy is taught and where the national curriculum will be applicable:

1. In an educational programme where a learner is studying for a vocational qualification (catering, forestry) or an academic subject qualification (art, sociology) but needs to, or simply is, improving their literacy/numeracy.

2. As the main part of their programme: they have attended training/ college/wherever they are being taught primarily to improve their literacy and/or numeracy.

Because the concept of *inclusive* education is so dominant throughout education, basic skills are often described as 'embedded within a programme' (taught as part of the course). Sometimes it is the case but more often it is an exaggeration. It is actually very difficult, if not impossible, for most tutors to effectively raise literacy standards at the same time as, for example, teaching students' how to change an oil filter or create puff pastry – although these practical tasks may be central to the main course on which they are studying.

Keeping to the examples used, it is therefore more realistic for the motor vehicle tutor's students to attend applied literacy classes in a classroom environment, say twice a week for two hours per session, with their tutor present and/or a specialist literacy tutor on-hand to support him or her. Similarly, the catering students and tutor need to come out of the kitchen to make an impact on their spelling, writing and reading but of course, can use topics within catering as a focus for improving their literacy. What is needed above all here is flexibility so that the most effective use is made of time, resources and expertise, keeping study enjoyable and relevant. Quite

TRTS THE RIGHT WORDS

often this may mean that a specialist literacy tutor takes the lead with the subject tutor in close support: spelling, reading and writing are not so much 'embedded' as flaunted. Often literacy or numeracy education takes place in the same location where most of this type of teaching happens within college/institution/centre and where there are specialist literacy/other resources – like multiple basic dictionaries- to hand (see the end of Section 1 for what resources I recommend).

These examples also underline an uncomfortable possible outcome of the increasing emphasis put upon standards, professionalism and Skills For Life: that those who teach or train the 16 + are increasing pressured or even forced, to work as a literacy/numeracy tutor *as well as a subject tutor*, with a minimum of support and training. This is a very undesirable but increasingly plausible scenario. As educationalists it should be obvious to us that compulsion cannot mix with learning in a sector that is built upon the notion of positive choice and improved life/life chances. It should also be obvious to all but the most ideologically (or is it financially?) driven, that literacy (English) and numeracy (maths) teaching are specialist areas and should thereby be recognised as such in terms of how teaching loads are allocated. To say that any teacher in the post-16 sector can teach English or maths is to completely undermine the whole notion of raising standards in these areas: if anybody can do it then why are so many adults experiencing difficulties? *The Right Words* advises that those who are new to this area build up their experience, their qualifications and skills in teaching literacy/ numeracy. This makes it a necessity that the institutions or organisations to whom they belong and who will ultimately benefit from their skills, give them the space, grace, and support to do so.

The Curriculum: Facts, Concepts and Organisation

The published, paper version is the main document for teachers and students. There are curricula covering the areas of numeracy, ESOL and literacy. A version entitled *Access For All* also accompanies these curricula and is about making all of these areas more accessible for students with disabilities and impairments.

Free Copies of all these are all available free from the Basic Skills Agency Admail 524 London WC1A 1BR. Tel. 0870 600 2400 www.basic-skills.co.uk.

The *Adult Literacy Core Curriculum* consists of:

- 144 pages, including a very useful Glossary and references

- 3 sections (in chronological order): Speaking and listening, Reading and, finally, Writing. Each section is colour-coded. Each 'page' opens as a double A4 spread and is normally read from left to right in terms of increasing detail - see below.

- An introduction that outlines the overall background to the standards and government strategy in this area.

- An extremely helpful general breakdown of 'The Progression Between Abilities' which outlines what a student should be able to do/ demonstrate at levels in their reading and separately, writing (ALCC pp. 10–11). To accompany this there is a breakdown of Reading and Writing sections within *The Curriculum*, in terms of progression, but using all the specific elements at each level (ALCC pp. 14–19).

The Focus 3-D Model and the Standards

A model of literacy and an official awareness of its own authoritative role, both underpin *The Curriculum* and are essential to understanding it and using it in a practical sense:

The 3-D Model

This is the idea, which runs through *The Curriculum*, that it is possible to 'differentiate between 3 dimensions in the process of reading and writing' (ALCC p.7). These dimensions are seen as dimensions of 'text', of 'sentence' and of 'word'.

There is no intention here to suggest that we only look at the 'word' or any other dimension solely when we are reading. In fact *The Curriculum* is keen to emphasise that this model 'recognises the complexity of the reading process' (ALCC p.7).

TRTS THE RIGHT WORDS

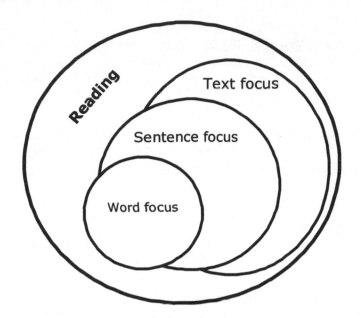

*Diagram of the 3-dimensional model of literacy
used in the curriculum*

The focus (dimension) model – see diagram above - is therefore an attempt to conceptualise the fact that when, for example, we read an article on 'New Restaurants in Manchester' by Frumpale Biggins we are thinking, often simultaneously...

text dimension: oh this is dull, nowhere near as good as that last article I read on Restaurants in Manchester: the descriptions of the restaurants are poor. It keeps on losing me and I don't know whom it is intended for: £100 for a main course, in a pub! The whole thing is badly written, the writer keeps jumping from place-to-place, it's not organised into locations or food types. Oh my coffee's gone cold...

sentence dimension: right next sentence...eyes scanning: "Afterwards we ate lobster marinated with black pudding jus at The Escargot Pub in central Manchester – it was marvellous." Is the writer boasting? What does 'jus' mean?

word dimension: "Frumpale Biggins" what an odd name – is he frumpy and likes ale? 'jus' is that French for juice? 'marinated' I can never spell this. 'Biggins' that sounds like 'Baggins': 'Bilbo Baggins' – the character from J.R Tolkein's *Lord of the Rings.*

The text focus, sentence focus and word focus model is therefore a practical way to impose order upon (to focus on) and therefore be able to organise, a cognitive process which slips between text, sentence, word, self and outside world.

The Standards

A key function of *The Curriculum* is setting out the National Standards. These standards are made up of skills and knowledge which, when enough are reached by a learner, add up to a level of competence, skills and capabilities. *The Curriculum* specifies what skills and what knowledge are required to reach this for each level and in doing so standardised what everyone means when they refer to 'Entry Level' or 'Level 2'.

By referring to the authority of the standards set out, in detail, in this publication the teacher knows exactly what a learner at, say, Level 1 should be able to do and what knowledge they will have. It follows that if this learner fails to meet all of these skills and knowledge then their teacher can identify where exactly they have failed and plan work to allow them to reach Level 1. Authority and national standardisation are key elements of this text.

Opposite, taken from *The Curriculum,* is a table that sets out these levels and their equivalent qualifications. The arrow, which I have added, denotes difficulty to achieve.

One significant aspect of the above table is in how it shows the equivalence of levels across the British education system. Achieving Level 1, for example, in Literacy/numeracy is shown to be equivalent to achieving Key Skills Level 1. There are as yet no official national literacy or numeracy qualifications available, although at the time of writing these were in the advanced stages of development.

　　　　　　　　TRTS THE RIGHT WORDS

National Levels (taken from the Curriculum, p.4)

	Literacy/Numeracy Level 2	Key Skills Level 2	National qualifications framework Level 2
National Curriculum Level 5 / National Curriculum Level 4	Literacy/Numeracy Level 1	Key Skills Level 1	National qualifications framework Level 1
National Curriculum Level 3	Literacy/Numeracy Entry 3		
National Curriculum Level 2	Literacy/Numeracy Entry 2		Entry Level
National Curriculum Level 1	Literacy/Numeracy Entry 1		

(DIFFICULTY ↑)

To put the above diagram in perspective, it is also worth considering that a GCSE, of any kind, is a Level 2 qualification. Often, during teacher training, when I explain this diagram to others, it creates a mild sense of surprise, even shock as the realisation occurs that *The Curriculum applies to adults who are below and in the case of entry level, well below GCSE English or maths in terms of the level of their literacy.* It is also worth commenting here on the distinction between achieving a qualification and achieving a level of competence set by the Standards in *The Curriculum*.

Occasionally, those who offer literacy or numeracy provision fall prey to this qualification fallacy, which is (typically) to muddle up passing a Key Skills Communication exam with the process of helping the student to progress with their spelling, reading and writing. They are not the same thing. The aim of literacy teaching in the 16+ area is to help the student progress with regards to their 'ability to read, write and speak in English and to use mathematics at a level necessary to function at work and in society in general.' (p.3 *The Curriculum)*. This is a far-wider remit than passing a qualification, hence the mention of 'employment' and 'society in general'. Any meaningful approach to raising the literacy of students who are over 16 must also include the notion that the student has autonomy in choosing why they want to improve their spelling, reading, writing and/or numeracy. They have to see the benefits for their life to be motivated and exams are not always part of this. Achieving qualifications – whether they are Key Skills, GCSE or City and Guilds – can be great motivators but should not dominate this process, turning it into a narrow race for grades. We should not be working to past exams papers but rather, towards a better future for the student- one where they can read, write and spell confidently for the rest of their life.

Organisation and Referencing

There are 4 main organising principles/formats that appear on each double page of *The Curriculum:*

- national standard, i.e. Entry 1 (E1), Entry 2 (E2), Entry 3 (E3), Level 1 (L1) and Level 2 (L2).

- curriculum focus sub-sections (i.e. word focus (w), text focus (t) and sentence focus (s).

- a curriculum reference which consists of the above preceded by W for Writing or R for Reading, e.g. Ww/L1, Rt/E3.

- finally there is a curriculum element number (e.g. ❶ *spell correctly words used most often in work, studies and* ...'). For example, the reference including the element number will appear as Ws/L1.1

Plus each double page also contains:

- guidance and/or sample activities which flesh out all of the above. These are often invaluable as they provide detailed advice about and examples of how to teach specific topics.

TRTS THE RIGHT WORDS

It is also the case that literacy is sub-divided into:

- reading comprehension
- writing composition
- vocabulary, word recognition and phonics
- spelling and handwriting

Try It Out

The best way to learn to use *The Curriculum,* especially in terms of gaining confidence with how it is organised and understanding its layout, plus recognising the kind of sub-skills that are assigned to each level in the standards, is to try to thoroughly apply it to a student whom you know/ teach. Ask yourself these questions about the student you select:

- What level are they at, generally, in the terms of the standards set out in *The Curriculum?* Does this match with what I already know of their abilities? Section 2 provides advice and offers a methodology for ascertaining this in terms of their spelling but this approach can shed light on more general abilities, strengths and weaknesses. The results of electronic-based initial assessment done at, or prior to enrolment, can be compared with *The Curriculum* and with your own knowledge.

- What Level do they want to progress to? What are their current strengths and weaknesses? This can start off at a fairly general level and, as you get more confident, can become highly focused with specific curriculum references assigned to the student's weaknesses and to their strengths.

- What would be my next plan of action: which elements from which focus sub-section would I select to take forward and work on over the next few weeks?

The final step would be to take this process forward onto the student's Individual Learning Plan (ILP). See the examples I give at the end of Section 4 on my sample learners Jill and Tony with regard to spelling.

Finally, it the case that *the activities, approaches and work needed to improve spelling and which are covered in the rest of this book, will allow you to cover at least a third of the overall content for literacy. That is 31 curriculum references, across all levels, which can be met* (See pp. 18 - 19 of *The Curriculum* for details of the full spread).

I hope this provides confidence for the reader.

Enjoyment and Interest

Enjoyment and interest are key aids to the learning process. While *The Right Words* relates the Adult Literacy Core Curriculum and ILPs to work on spelling, I hope that it also suggests ways in which the topic can be made interesting and enjoyable for both learner and teacher. Liberal use of humour, images and accessible topics vastly improves learning – especially in terms of motivation to progress.

Wherever possible use the student's personal interests as a generator for tasks, assignments and exercises. Make full use of television, films, the internet, magazines, visits, email, the lyrics of music and College/local Magazines. The tutor can also get students to create classroom decorations/visually appealing work in the form of word-charts, word-families, suffixes and prefixes. The tutor can also ask students to create displays of topic-words (football, music, etc.) with images, and cannibalise magazines to extend vocabulary and look at unusual spellings or create collages from newspapers where they have to create the headlines. Work on rhyme and rhythm in language and use of mind-maps, colours and spidergrams whilst teaching spelling rules and word-families is very useful (see the recommended book by Tony Buzan on the reading list at the end of this section on Mind Maps and other learning aids).

In short, avoid repetitive worksheets and, instead, rigorously teach spelling through activities that have some imagination and that give some pleasure to student (and tutor). This holds true for all literacy teaching and the educational phrase 'multi-sensory' teaching (teaching using all the senses) is actually a lot less specialist when considered from this view. Using all the senses, using colour, humour and imagination is actually just good teaching.

Resources and Reading Required

Many of the resources required are not specific to spelling but they are required to teach a range of literacy (and even numeracy) skills. Unfortunately, it is amazing how many of those teaching in a post-school setting do not have basic resources like a private room. In compiling this list I am presuming that the tutor has never taught before and is starting from scratch. Most resources below are essential but a few, like Scrabble, are optional:

- a private room for 1:1 work and a larger teaching room for group work
- tape recorders and/or dictaphones
- Scrabble, junior and standard
- blank flash cards
- Shorter Oxford English Dictionary, a thesaurus (not Roget's: use a simpler version, alphabetically organised) and an ACE Dictionary (see the reading list that follows)
- acetate overlays and non-permanent pens, cotton wool and solvent for cleaning the overlays
- adult-scale tables and chairs
- a large pack of coloured felt tip pens
- extra wide/wide feint ruled paper and a selection of pastel-coloured paper (pastel coloured paper is far easier to read on than white for most people but particularly for those with dyslexia or visual problems)
- copies of the Literacy and Numeracy Adult Curricula and Access for All. These are available free from the Basic Skills Agency Admail 524 London WC1A 1BR. Tel. 0870 600 2400
- a range of suitable magazines and some recent newspapers (published within the last month)
- access to computers with a spellchecker, word-processing facilities and the internet. If used selectively, the internet is a fantastic tool for teaching literacy – look for sites on word-origins for example.
- access to tea and coffee. It's amazing how the prospect of a cup of coffee can enthuse a tired student

In addition to the above resources, the following books are recommended for the tutor to read and refer to:

- *ACE Spelling Dictionary* (various publishers, the teacher though has to read the introduction/directions and familiarise themselves with use before recommending to learners).
- Basic Skills Agency: *The Spelling Pack*, London: 1988.
- Beve Hornsby and Julie Pool: *Alpha To Omega Activity Packs* 1 to 3, Heinemann, Oxford: 1993.
- Buzan, Tony and Barry: *The Mind Map Book*, BBC Worldwide Limited, London: Rev. ed. 2000.
- Cynthia Klein and Robin Millar: *Making Sense of Spelling*, SENJIT Institute of Education, London: 1986.
- Cynthia Klein and Robin Millar: *Unscrambling Spelling*, Hodder and Stoughton, London: 1990.
- Cynthia Klein: *Diagnosing Dyslexia*, The Basic Skills Agency, London: 1993.
- Edward Lear: *The Book of Nonsense and Nonsense Songs*, Penguin Popular Classics: 1996.
- Elizabeth Wood: *Exercise Your Spelling*, Hodder and Stoughton, London: Rev. ed.1990.
- Elizabeth Wood: *Strengthen your Spelling*, Hodder and Stoughton, London: 1996.
- Lucy Cowdery: *Spelling Rulebook*, TRTS Publishing, Wrexham. 2001.
- Paula Morse: *The Kingston Cursive Handwriting Programme*, (part of the Teaching Reading Through Spelling Programme), TRTS Publishing, Wrexham. 2001.
- R.C. Phillips: *The Skills of Handwriting*, R.C. Phillips Ltd, London: 1976.
- R. Sassoon and G.S.E. Briem: *Teach Yourself Better Handwriting*, Hodder and Stoughton, London: 1993.
- The Skills for Life Teaching Qualifications Framework: A User's Guide DfES Publications, Nottingham: 2003.
- Wide Ranging Achievement Test (or WRAT) Jastak Associates, New York: 1993 (a statistically rigorous assessment for reading, writing and arithmetic).

TRTS THE RIGHT WORDS

Section 2: GETTING STARTED

Assessment & Planning

This Section outlines the assessment of need and planning that is required
before spelling can be tackled. It outlines how to:

- Diagnose a pattern of misspellings with a systematic analysis based
  around common weaknesses. An example of writing by Tony and Jill,
  our two case studies, is given and their spelling difficulties are analysed.
- Plan a spelling programme on the basis of this insight. Aims and
  objectives for dealing with Tony and Gill's problems are set out. Draft
  plans of a spelling programme with them are included in this Section.
  Their final formal Individual Learning Plans (ILPs) are given at the end
  of Section 4.

The Process

Taken down to its bare bones the whole process of improving spelling is
fairly simple:

- a piece of handwritten, uncorrected work is analysed for errors
- a pattern of errors is identified
- planning is done on how to tackle weaknesses and make the most of
  strengths
- the plan is negotiated with the student before being formally written
  on their ILP
- the plan is implemented
- progress is reviewed after a realistic period

Where skill, judgement and experience make a difference is in identifying what kinds of errors are happening and in how particular strategies/strategy combinations can be used to tackle them.

Focusing on learners' problems might not seem like the most obvious starting point. It is, however, essential. Learner and tutor need to look at their patterns of mistakes and attack these using the learner's personal strengths. This is the essence of the 'teaching to strengths' approach often mentioned on teacher training courses and it is especially effective when improving spelling. The best way to look at a learner's strengths and weaknesses in spelling is to have an uncorrected, handwritten piece of their writing on a topic with which they are familiar. Before analysing a students' work it is however important to ask three questions:

1. Has an assessment already been done of a students' spelling?

   Although this might not be sufficient to provide all the information needed, the assessment can at least offer additional examples of misspellings. If it is Curriculum Linked, like the Basic Skills Agency Literacy and Numeracy assessment, then the information can be invaluable in the next step: designing a spelling programme that fits in with wider progress in the Curriculum.

2. How do they feel about their spelling?

   Talk to them, as informally as possible. This can be a goldmine of useful information for a teacher. Has spelling always been a problem? Are problems connected with a particular topic or area? An informal discussion can reveal the extent of problems, give clues as to patterns of misspellings and above all offer a holistic insight into their particular strengths and weaknesses. At a later date all this can be invaluable in designing a programme that fits their needs..

3. Is any suitable uncorrected, handwritten writing already available?

   If not then this needs to be obtained. A learner at E1 or E2 especially might be reluctant to provide this, worrying about the standard of what they will produce. It is especially important that the teacher

TRTS THE RIGHT WORDS

explains that he or she is looking for mistakes so that they can know what words to work on with the learner. It can also be explained that the tutor will also help the learner see their own patterns of errors and in time overcome them.

It must be emphasised that the learner should <u>not</u> correct their mistakes on what must be a hand written text. This is occasionally very difficult but the teacher must stick to this request! Only learners with physical or visual impairments can be exempt from producing a handwritten piece for assessment (see 'Access for All' for advice on making the written elements of the Curriculum more accessible to these learners).

Wt/E2.1 asks that the learner be taught to *"use written words and phrases to record or present information"* that is *"fit for intended purpose"* and that the writer selects the best organisation and style for the context, audience and purpose'. An example is given of *"compose and write short texts for different audiences in their daily life"*.

As a basis for misspelling analysis, and as an initial assignment, the teacher could ask the learner to write about a personal interest. This could be from a vast range: a TV programme; a football team; favourite foods and why; a singer or musician/band – the list is endless. Discuss this assignment with the learner. Those with low confidence or at E1/E2 may need a writing frame. Writing frames can be quickly drawn up on a word-processor, with the learner actually contributing to the prompts. (See the example on the next page).

The text that the learner is asked to produce should ideally, be around one A4 side. For learners at E1/E2 this can be a challenge but do try to obtain as much material as possible. The more free writing available, the more problems - and potential strategies to tackle them – become available to analyse and work on.

At a later date, after progress, this assignment can be re-written using all the skills that the learner has gained across the literacy Curriculum. A variety of Curriculum elements can be achieved through this: Wt/E2.1, Ws/E2.1, 2 and 3; Wt/E3.1, 2, 3 and 4. With development the piece can contribute to achieving **word**, **text** and **sentence** focus elements at L1 and L2. Most importantly this piece of writing can provide the teacher and learner with a clear indication of positive progress at all three levels.

For those wishing an evaluation of a learners' spelling abilities that is statistically rigorous then the Wide Ranging Achievement Test (or WRAT, Jastak Associates 1993) can be used. This test provides a standardised score which means that the student's ability in spelling can be compared with his or her peers in a precise way. For most purposes, however, an uncorrected, handwritten composition on a topic of interest provides a more holistic basis for assessment by the teacher.

Here is an example of a writing frame that can be used as an initial assignment:

MY FAVOURITE FILM

My favourite film is:

It stars:

It is about:

What happens is:

I like it because:

At the end:

TRTS THE RIGHT WORDS

Analysing a Pattern of Errors

Analysing the resulting text can seem daunting for those new to literacy teaching. It actually soon become apparent where and with what frequency the students is making errors, close reading of their text by the teacher is key here to identifying and classifying errors. Common errors include:

- Double letters: **assess, programme, bill**.

- Silent letter combinations: **gh** in **thought**; **caracter** rather than **character** and also vowel combinations in words such as **receive**, **foal**, and **cough**.

- Sequencing: **piad**, rather than **paid**, **hieght** rather than **height**.

- Missing letters: **belif** rather than **belief**, **meanin** rather than 'meaning'.

- Logical phonetic alternative: words which follow English spelling conventions and that would be 'acceptable':
eggample for **example**; **serface** for **surface**.

Designing A Spelling Programme

The next step is to design a spelling programme around the learners' individual needs and relevant Word Focus elements from the Curriculum. The Individual Learning Plan (ILP) is the key document that should be used to record this.

- The spelling programme, centered on the Word Focus level of the Curriculum and specific elements within Word Focus, should be integrated into the learners' overall learning plan for literacy. Planning for progression in spelling, in phonics and in vocabulary (described as part of Word Focus by the Curriculum) is recorded on the ILP as a part of planning for progress in text focus and sentence focus. Activities, assignments and progress recorded later on the plan should also reflect this integration.

The Adult Literacy Core Curriculum is explicit about the need for integration. It emphasises that *'It is critical that the adult literacy core Curriculum is used in (an) integrated way. It is not a list of separate and discrete activities. Text - Sentence – and Word focus elements must all be covered.'* (p.8, ALCC)

Learning around the words themselves, their structure, spelling and individual character is enriched and contextualised by this integrated, interdependent approach. The ILP is, however, an individual learning plan and on the basis of this it is sometimes the case that the ILP reflects the heavy significance that the learner places on tackling spelling key words crucial to their life or study.

For learners with more extensive needs it is often practical to have one ILP that deals solely with their spelling and other related word focus topics, otherwise it is just not possible to physically fit the information required on the ILP!

In this particular case it is important that the Spelling Programme ILP makes, albeit brief, reference to an *overall* ILP that plans, records and monitors progress at sentence and text focus levels.

Tony and Jill's final ILPs are given at the end of Section 4 and while focusing on spelling and elements from word focus, they make reference to other elements across the Curriculum which fit in with/are met by the objectives set out in the ILP. For a busy teacher this not only saves time but also ensures that topics are covered in a meaningful way and comprehensive way.

An Effective Programme
Following Klein (1990), any effective programme needs to be:

- Meaningful: based around the words that the student needs to use in their own life or in study.

- Individualised: words should be approached using strategies that fit with the students' own strengths but with their weaknesses borne

 **THE RIGHT WORDS**

in mind: teach to strengths but be aware of weaknesses. For example, Ww/L2.2 in the *Adult Literacy Core Curriculum* requires that learners 'understand how knowledge of word roots, prefixes and suffixes can support spelling'. Dyslexic learners or those with visual weaknesses are likely to find working on visual elements of words difficult. This difficulty needs to be acknowledged, if possible overcome or different approaches used.

- <u>Multi-sensory</u>: involve all the senses, especially with beginner learners at E1, E2 or those with more severe problems.

- <u>Structured</u>: this allows steady progression to take place and ensures they retain the correct spellings over the long term. It also allows for effective review of learning and improves learner confidence.

- <u>At a Learner's Pace</u>: do not overload the programme, the student should learn to correctly spell no more than ten words per week – the majority of which should be familiar. Review their learning together and ensure they retain correct spellings by regular informal testing.

It is also important that the spelling programme is taught through a variety of teaching methods. This is especially important at L1 and L2 as learners are expected at Ww/L2.1: to '*know and apply a range of methods...to help learn and remember spellings*'. Awareness of how others learn to spell develops their awareness of what works for them.

One - to - one work is essential on spelling but this should take place alongside pair work, small group work and on common issues, and whole group teaching (see Section 5 and Section 3 and Section 4 for examples of a range of spelling methods which fit in with these different teaching modes).

Working with their peers allows common problems to be aired, shared and tackled. Students can support and encourage each other as they progress through the Curriculum. Teachers need to design activities and sessions that allow for the different abilities of learners (differentiation). As was emphasised in the Introduction, the best way to meet differing abilities is by designing activities that are fun, flexible and not over-reliant on completing worksheets.

TEACHING THE POST-16 TO SPELL   29

At this point, if not before, it also becomes apparent if the learner has profound difficulties with spelling. Dyslexia and other related specific learning difficulties usually cause major, lifelong, problems with spelling. This is a symptom of a deeper 'difficulty with words'. While this book is not about dyslexia, the disorder cannot be ignored when tackling spelling with adult learners. At the end of this section I offer some brief advice on how to deal with this issue, including a methodology for referral.

My favourit Car

The new Hondah Civik is my favourit car. It has a sofisticated engine. and is totaly cool. It would be great too go for a drive in one – they look damn cool. The engine is a 2.2 liter turbo charged monster. The car costs 22 thousand too by. My favourit color is padle blue, althogh the silver-metalic is good too. They showde one at the birmingham Car Show, which i went to with Colege. it was really cool, we were alowed too go their by our key skil tutor. we went by coach althogh i would hav lined too have driven down there on the motor-way in a new Honta Civik. That woot have been cool.

Tony's Free Writing: An Example

Spelling Case Study: TONY

Tony is a student on a Motor Mechanic course. Although there is a focus on practical work he has some course written work. He is also enrolled on a Key Skills course at Level 1. His course tutors have noticed that he has problems with spelling: especially words of over two syllables and more technical words needed for study. His handwriting is often poor with irregular or badly formed letter construction and uneven size. Lack of practise, lack of confidence and poorly developed skills often prevent him from expressing himself in writing fully. His reading of course-related materials is basic but functional, although he does report 'missing words' sometimes when he reads and sometimes losing his place. Tony has just turned 17. Due to family problems, truancy and exclusion he missed much of his schooling between the ages of 13 – 16, he also missed some of his primary schooling.

Analysis

Look carefully at Tony's free writing (see facing page). What points are immediately noticeable?

- His poor handwriting and uneven/awkward letter formation.

- His phonetic spelling, e.g. **sofisticated**; **Hondah**; **liter.**

- His limited expression and repetition, e.g. **cool.**

- Several homophones - **wood** rather than **would**; **too** rather than **to**).

- Missing or uncertain double letters, e.g. **metalic**; **colege.**

- Missing or incorrectly ordered letters, e.g. **pael**; **showede**; **hav**.
- Grammatical errors, e.g. **i** for **I**.

- He can write very simple sentences using a capital letter and full stop.

- The passage, largely, makes sense.

- He can write with enthusiasm.

The fact that Tony misses out or gets confused with double letters, mixes up **le**, **ae** and generally spells phonetically, indicates that he has visual weaknesses in his spelling.

This observation is reinforced by his comment about 'missing words' when he reads and losing his place (tracking). The disordered nature of his handwriting indicates possible weaknesses in his fine-motor control. Having said this he does admit to 'hardly ever' writing before the course he is currently on and he did use blank rather than lined paper – lined paper might have helped him regulate the size and direction of his letters. He also typically, used a cheap chewed biro!

Work With Tony: A Plan
Over the course of an academic year:

Aims:

1. Improve the quality of handwriting, particularly letter size and formation.
2. Improve his use of double letters: e.g. **ll** (**college**); **mm** (**common**, **comment**).
3. Understand and correct common homophones: **their** and **there**; **to** and **too**; **hear** and **here.**
4. Reinforce his knowledge of spellings he already knows: **Birmingham**; **engine**; **monster.**
5. Pick out and correctly spell the important words for his study at college: **metallic** (paint); **chassis**; **carburettor**; **college**; **Key Skills**.
6. Improve his vocabulary by showing him how to confidently spell new words.

TRTS THE RIGHT WORDS

Objectives (how the aims will be met)

<u>Handwriting</u>: Exercises on letter formation; trying different pens; looking at posture and how the pen is held.

<u>Double Letters:</u> Pick out double letter words; look at common formations 'll', 'mm' and 'ss', include 1 or 2 double letter words each week in the spelling programme.

<u>Homophones</u>: Teach separately, include them in the Spelling Programme.

<u>Phonetic Spelling</u>: Use Tony's strengths in phonics to look at syllables (Ww/E2). Basic concepts and exercises, stressed and unstressed syllables, open and closed, **l** and **le** endings, e.g.

> /a/ and multiple choice spellings, e.g. **wait** or **weight**?
> **ch** saying /k/
> **que** saying' /k/
> **ch** saying /sh/

Use phonics and other methods to work on irregular words and suffixes/prefixes.

<u>Important Words:</u> Words he needs to know at college can be used to reveal spelling patterns, spelling rules, semantic word families.

<u>New Words:</u> Tony should identify a minimum of 3 new words each week with meanings and put these into a personal spelling dictionary

He should write a little every day and be set extra regular written work on high-interest topics (new car models etc) on top of his coursework. He will start the LOOK, COVER, WRITE, CHECK method and overall progress will be reviewed regularly (every 6 weeks).

Movement   14/1/03

How you worked with your own skills in movement

To make sure I worked with my own skills ~~in~~ in movement ~~with~~ I used all the space ~~best~~ appropritly. I thought it would be ~~best~~ best to ~~move~~ move the ~~chess~~ chairs away from the table so we could move around more quickly and safer. I toke out moves that did not fit for me. For example I added a move ment for the line "The kind of put where yet'dd weasal assemble". I was going to stand up and bend over to ~~emphises~~ the "~~~~ holes" bit. But then I realsed it would not fit in as there was some think going on on the other side of the set at the same time.

I also worked with others. Me and Francesca ~~~~ stood to ~~anthor~~ nasty as if we were two boys . For the line "envying their lives". This worked realy well as I was envying Francesca carater it realy showed in our movemets. Before I started I did a full body and vocal warm up. This is very important because I have to be 100% ready to preforme to the best of my ability. And making sure I'am preforming all the movements.

I Practised the whole piece over + over agin and in different way's. For example

Jill's Free Writing: An Example

TRTS THE RIGHT WORDS

Spelling Case Study: JILL

Jill is a student enrolled on a BTEC Drama course (level 3). Her tutor reported that she was finding it hard to spell many of the words she needed to know. Jill is a motivated student with no obvious history of difficulty with written expression: she has a GCSE English at Grade C. The example given is a write-up of a performance.

Analysis

Points immediately noticeable:

- Jill is obviously trying to stretch her vocabulary and attempt (without a dictionary) some longer multi-syllabic words such as appropriately, movement and emphasises but is having a poor success rate.

- Despite spelling problems she is able to produce writing of a reasonable quantity – unlike Tony there was plenty of handwritten coursework to choose from for analysis.

- Notice her spelling of 'appropriately' (**apropitly**); 'perform' (**preforme**); 'enjoying' (**enjying**); and 'emphasises' (**ephises**). In all of these cases she is missing out important sounds (phonemes) within the word – usually vowels, or getting the vowels in the wrong place.

- Jill is also making some other errors in terms of sentence and grammar use: Grammatically '**Me and Francesca**' should for example be '**Francesca and I**'

- What the analysis does not disclose is that Jill has reasonable editing skills. All the words underlined are words that I asked her to pick out as words she felt were wrongly spelled and her final (word-processed) version of the piece had only two spelling errors.

- The facts that: Jill is on a course requiring relatively sophisticated written expression (a BTEC); that she is obviously trying hard to grasp the level of vocabulary required by her study; that she has reasonable editing skills, all disclose the aims of our work with her.

Work With Jill. A Plan

Aims

1. An aim of work with her is to 'unblock' her written expression and to allow her to fully participate/achieve her BTEC Drama in terms of written work required. Work on spelling is the means to this end.

2. Secondary aim: any other spellings she needs for everyday life.

Objectives (how the aims will be met)

Vowels: Concepts and use of vowels, long and short.

Syllables: Explain the concept of syllables and practise at splitting words into syllables (syllabication)

Irregular Words: Practice irregular words.

Dictionary: Start personal dictionary (course words)

Grammar: E..g. 'Francesca and I'

Sentence Use: Concept and use of complex sentences

New Words: Improve her vocabulary by showing her how to confidently spell new words and put these into a personal spelling dictionary

Look, Cover, Write: She will start the Look, Cover, Write, Check method and review overall progress regularly..

Taking Stock
At this stage and before moving on, to look at what strategies can be effective the teacher should have:

- Checked if any prior assessment of spelling is available.

- Received an example of free writing from the student for analysis.

- Identified the students' individual patterns of errors from this text.

- Negotiated a list of key words the students wants to learn to spell and spoken to them about their spelling.

- Considered how the learner's individual strengths, weaknesses and overall needs can be incorporated into a spelling programme.

- Considered how to record the students' personal aims onto the ILP, integrating work on these and on specific word focus elements, with the wider objectives of the *Adult Literacy Core Curriculum*, i.e. work at word focus elements like spelling should be related to sentence focus and text focus too.

- Started to examine what strategies are available to directly tackle spelling.

- Given the fact that Jill has not missed portions of her education, is obviously motivated but is nevertheless missing out sounds in her writing (phonemes), then her tutor should refer her for a dyslexia assessment.

Dyslexia: What is it? What Can I Do?

Dyslexia is a specific learning difficulty that affects an individual's processing of language. Estimates vary widely as to the percentage of the population whom are dyslexic, however, according to the British Dyslexia Association 10% of the population are affected. Of this total figure 4% are severely dyslexic and 6% have mild-to-moderate dyslexia. The Dyslexia Institute provide a good definition of the condition:

> *Dyslexia causes difficulties in learning to read, write and spell. Short-term memory, mathematics, concentration, personal organisation and sequencing may also be affected.*
>
> *Dyslexia usually arises from a weakness in the processing of language-based information. Biological in origin, it tends to run in families, but environmental factors also contribute.*
>
> *Dyslexia can occur at any level of intellectual ability. It is not the result of poor motivation, emotional disturbance, sensory impairment or lack of opportunities, but it may occur alongside any of these.*
>
> *The effects of dyslexia can be largely overcome by skilled specialist teaching and the use of compensatory strategies.*
>
> *The Dyslexia Institute 2002*

Spelling in particular and writing generally are the most obvious places where dyslexia can be revealed. This is why awareness of the issue is important for those teaching spelling and literacy in post-16 learning. The piece of free writing that the student hands in initially for you to assess might be where this issue first appears.

What To Do If A Student May Be Dyslexic

- Talk to the student, in private, about their spelling and writing generally. Be supportive and listen carefully, those with dyslexia have

 THE RIGHT WORDS

often had a very negative experience of education. You may be the first teacher that they can go on to develop a positive relationship with. If they missed a lot of school it might be possible that their problems are simply lost education time and/or the fact they do not write or read regularly.

• Assess whether their spelling mistakes are persistent, severe and accompanied by other problems such as: confusing 'b' and 'd', 'm' and 'n'; poor organisation; and poor concentration. Very poor handwriting with badly formed letters is often a telling sign of possible dyslexia. Spelling everything as it is said (phonically) but showing awareness of common spelling rules in English indicates that the person is probably not dyslexic.

• With the student, visit the British Dyslexia Association and Dyslexia Institute websites. They offer excellent advice and on-line screening.

• If you are still uncertain about the student or still concerned contact your Learning Support Department/person or contact the British Dyslexia Association directly for details on what to do next.

Section Summary

Assess
• Formally and informally.
• What are their strengths and weaknesses? Teach to strengths.
• Identify a pattern of errors from a piece of their handwritten, uncorrected handwriting.

Verbally Negotiate
Verbally negotiate a spelling plan with the learner which follows their priorities. When working to the *Adult Literacy Core Curriculum* this should aim towards achievement of elements within word focus, principally by improving their spelling in words they have chosen. It should be designed to build on their previous knowledge and aim towards achievement of the targets you have set together; that is achievement, ultimately, of the appropriate standard (E1, E2, E3, L1, L2). What do they need to learn to achieve this? What is realistic and possible given their current level and

time available? How might work on spelling fit in with ongoing or future sentence focus and text focus work?

Formally Record

Formally record the learners' aims on their ILP. Plan to record and evidence progress in spelling. If possible, make brief reference to the Word Focus element set as objectives. Learners with more substantial needs may need a separate ILP. If they do, ensure it is fully related to their main one.

Note: A student with persistent/severe difficulties in spelling and reading may have dyslexia – see the sub-heading earlier in this section.

The Next Step

With all of this information available the teacher can now start to consider and select strategies available to tackle spelling. Graphophonics is a good topic to start with and this is the subject of the next section.

TRTS THE RIGHT WORDS

Section 3: GRAPHOPHONICS

Graphophonics
Why Teach It?
How To Teach It and an Overview of Topics
Graphophonical Topics in the Curriculum
Three Topics in Focus
Section Summary

Graphophonics

Graphophonics is the point at which the oral world of language and that of written expression interact. Many individuals with poor literacy or dyslexia are articulate verbally, yet for all this they have severe problems transferring this knowledge into writing and spelling. For them it is as if their weaknesses in the written realm are compensated for in their oral skills.

To accurately spell a word we must be able to combine the right sound(s) with the right letter shape. Sound and visual appearance must work in harmony: the system that allows this is known as the graphophonic system (often abbreviated to 'phonics'). Letter shapes are known as graphemes and letter sounds are collectively known as phonemes.

Inaccurate spelling often stems from the fact that a learners' graphophonic system is either partial or ineffective - or both. Without the right sounds/sound combinations tied to their correct respective letter/letter combinations, and with consistency, then spelling becomes inconsistent or even arbitrary.

A complication here is that in English there is no simple one-to-one correspondence: there are 26 letters in the alphabet but 44 different possible phonemes. To make matters worse there are just over 100 different ways to spell all 44 phonemes.

An important factor to remember is that graphophonics is a topic rather than a single approach: it is less a way to 'do' a specific thing and more of an area of study from a viewpoint with many approaches that can be used.

Why Teach It?

The main reason for teaching graphophonics is to allow the learner to combine graphemes and phonemes in a consistent and effective way. The goal is that eyes and ears, sight and sound, letter shapes and letter sounds/sound combinations, work in a co-ordinated way to produce more accurate spelling. Practice and theory, 'doing it' and 'understanding' - the why - need to combine closely through exercises and teaching. Effective, consistent use of the alphabet, discriminating letter sounds and recognition of syllables needs to be tied to intellectual understanding of, for example, the function of vowels and digraphs.

How To Teach It: An Overview

The vast majority of post 16 learners will have some use of their graphophonic system. The aim then when teaching this topic should be to help them pin down, extend or repair their own knowledge, rather than have them re-learn the whole system. With this in mind, what follows is an overview of the whole topic, tied to the *Adult Literacy Core Curriculum*. To help this area seem less daunting, advice is also given on teaching 3 selected sub topics.

It is important that graphophonics is taught in a structured way and that learners are introduced to sub-topics, such as syllables, in a sequential manner. Do not move on to new areas before being certain that the learner has grasped and has had success in an area – although work can carry on concurrently if a learner demonstrates some competency. Within the study of syllables for example, make sure that the student understands what one is and is shown a short word divided into syllables before they are asked to break up a word into its component syllables.

Some rule-led teaching is required but over reliance on rules is likely to confuse and bore students in equal measure. Many spelling 'rules' are often not rules in the accepted sense anyway, as exceptions and anomalies exist: I prefer the term 'guide' or 'pattern' as students are alerted to the fact that exceptions might exist and are encouraged to check their spelling.

Pattern is a particularly useful way of recasting rules This is partly because recognition of letter-sound patterns is a key skill for effective spelling. Getting students to *identify patterns* is a key goal of teaching within graphophonics and within work on spelling more generally.

TRTS THE RIGHT WORDS

In the sub-topics below it is important that learners can demonstrate their skills in <u>identifying</u>, <u>reading</u> and <u>legibly writing</u> before they move on. Practicing all three of these skills correctly is also a requirement of the *Adult Literacy Core Curriculum.*

For example, the learner should be able to consistently recognise a long vowel such as '**oo**', read words containing '**oo**', like **door**, and be able to correctly write words like **door**, **look** and so on, before they move on to the next topic.

It is also important, in what follows, that the student has grasped some of the fundamental points, like the alphabet, before they move on to more complex concepts such as suffixes: clear, steady progress is key to success in this topic.

Graphophonical Topics in the Curriculum

The Alphabet (Ww/E1)
Alphabet familiarity, discrimination and ability to legibly write lower case letters – particularly problem letters e.g. **m, n, p** and **q.**

Capital letters (Ww/E1, Wt/E1)
The ability to recognise capital letters and distinguish them from lower case writing; the ability to legibly write capital letters.

Simple Vowels (Ww/E1)
Vowels and consonants: **a e i o u** – can the student identify vowels in 5 familiar words?

Dipgraphs (Ww/E1)
Recognise consonant dipgraphs: **sh, ch** and **th.**

Blends and Consonant clusters (Ww/E1)
Initial consonant blends as required from this list: **bl, br, cl, cr, dr, dw,**

fl, fr, gl, gr, pl, pr, sc, scr, sk, sl, sm, sn, sp, spl, spr, squ, st, str, sw, tw, tr, thr, shr
Common word end clusters as required from this list: : ld, nd, lk, sk, lp, mp, sp, ct, ft, lt, nt, pt, st, xt, lf, nch, lth

Vowels (Ww/E2)
Discriminate read and spell long vowel phonemes **ee, ai, ie, oa, oo.**
Discriminate read and spell vowel phonemes **oo, ar, oy, ow.**
Discriminate read and spell the common vowel phonemes **air, or, er.**
Long vowels: a – consonant – rule.

M or N? (Ww/E2)
Which one is required? **m** or **n**?

Hard and soft sounds (Ww/E2)
hard and soft sounds: **cri<u>ck</u>et**.

Syllables (Ww/E2)
Basic concepts and exercises, stressed and unstressed syllables, open and closed, **l** and **le** endings.

/a/ and multiple choice spellings e.g. **wait** or **weight**?
ch saying /k/
que saying' /k/
ch saying /sh/

Suffixes and Prefixes (Ww/E3)
Whilst teaching this topic give students a colour code for discriminating suffixes from prefixes e.g. 'blue for suffixes', 'red for prefixes'. Get them to use this code when completing exercises.

Simple or common suffixes: -**ful**, **ly**, -**less** camp**ed**, play**ing**
Prefixes: **un-, dis-, de-, re, pre** -school, **post**-college.

Word endings (Ww/E3)
Examples: **ery, ary** and **ory, sion, ssion**.

Homophones, 'confusibles' and silent letters (Ww/E3)
Silent **gh**, **their** and **there**, but remember to teach homophones seperately,

i.e., **their** should be looked at in a separate session from **there** as teaching them together will confuse the student. This can also be taught at a more basic level and used in conjunction with a spelling programme that fits an individual's needs (see Section 4 and the LOOK, COVER, WRITE, CHECK method).

Advanced suffixes and prefixes (Ww/E3 and above)

Words such as **contradictory**, **chronological**, **microscope** - any other technical words required by the learners' course or employment. These can be taught on a 1:1 basis and when learners are confident, a group session to share knowledge and demonstrate new skills can be arranged.

Should the teacher want to draw on some pre-made exercises and resources *Alpha To Omega*, the *Basic Skills Agency Spelling Pack* and Elizabeth Wood's *Exercise Your Spelling* and *Strengthen Your Spelling* all have excellent graphophonic exercises and worksheets that progress through these sub-topics. The *Spelling Rulebook* by Lucy Cowdery (published by TRTS) is another comprehensive reference book covering the phonic principles which recur in English.

Graphophonics: Three Topics in Focus

Here are three particular topics for which detailed teaching instruction is given.

The Alphabet (Ww/E1)

Without clarity on this learners will struggle with later concepts such as digraphs or syllables. Work on the alphabet with primarily be with students at E1 but even advanced students may have occasional difficulties with certain letters, often distinguishing between **d** and **b**, **m** and **n**, **p** and **q**. Such difficulties can be a sign of dyslexia. Do not work on these problem letters together, e.g. **m** and **n**, instead teach them separately. Find out which letters are a problem for your learner and focus on them as well as learning the alphabet as an overall sequence.

Because it can be an emotionally sensitive area, the alphabet is best taught on a one-to-one (1:1) basis. Some privacy is preferable. For the same reasons do not get learners to recite the alphabet parrot-fashion – unless they want to.

A good multisensory approach (an approach involving all the senses (see Introduction) is to print out the alphabet <u>in colours</u>, ideally so that every letter has a slightly different shade, e.g.

a b c d e f g h i j k l m n o p q r s t u w x y z

(Print the letters on a single line in Comic Sans size **18** points)

1. Point to a problem letter,
2. Get the learner to close their eyes and visualise this letter.
3. Can they 'see' it?
4. Can they see any letters next to it – which ones?
5. Next ask them to say it and then say a familiar word containing this letter.
6. Ask them to write the letter down and then the word containing the letter.
7. Next ask them to read the word they have written. Ask them to memorise the letter and the word they have picked e.g. **m** for **money**.
8. Tell them to put their work away and have a short coffee break or work on another topic.

When they return:

1. Get them to point to the letter in the alphabet and say it - what other letters is it next to?
2. Can they think of any words which contain the letter?
3. Can they write the letter out, then the word out and say them at the same time?

Obtain a thin piece of card (e.g. 4 cm high x 30 cm long) . Cut a 15mm wide window in the card, roughly in the middle, which can neatly show *only* 3 letters at a time. Place the coloured alphabet beneath this card. The card can be slid over the coloured printed alphabet to mask off all but three of the letters.

TRTS THE RIGHT WORDS

g h i

Ask the student to say the three letters they see. This allows learners to focus on three letters at a time rather than be distracted by the whole alphabet in front of them.

Get them to predict the next three letters. After time, chunks of letters can be linked up to start work on the whole sequence of the alphabet, this is important for using a dictionary later.

Note: The choice of font is important. **Arial** and **Comic Sans** are both far easier to read for most people than, say, **Times New Roman**. Present your learner with the alphabet in different fonts. Which one is easiest to read?

Reading can be used as a focus for problem letters and work on the alphabet: e.g. 'How many times can you see **"n"** in this article on the internet? – pick them out using a highlighter and count, look at each word containing '**n**'.

Handwriting is also implicated in problems with the alphabet because it Involves effective co-ordination of a learner's graphophonic system and their motor skills. Work on handwriting conversely, can greatly improve their graphophonic system. Learners with poor letter formation should be strongly encouraged to work on their handwriting.

After examination of a piece of his free writing and questioning on the alphabet, it emerged that Tony, our E1 case-study student had problems with writing and recognising '**n**' and '**r**'. (see Section 2 and Section 4). Studying the alphabet and study of these letters in particular was tied to work on his handwriting.

Once the alphabet has been consolidated as a topic, then the way is free to move on to digraphs and blends.

Vowels (Ww/E2)

The Curriculum specifies that this area covers the ability to:

Discriminate, read and spell long vowel phonemes **ee, ai, ie, oa oo**
Discriminate, read and spell vowel phonemes **oo, ar, oy, ow**
Discriminate, read and spell the common vowel phonemes **air, or, er**

This can be taught in many ways but a good start consists of reminding them that vowels come in short forms and re-reminding them of any previous sessions on short vowels. Giving a summary of previous learning in

the same area aids recall of what they already know and sets the scene for new, related knowledge.

Next, give an example of a short vowel (e.g. l**o**t)

Next introduce the concept of a long vowel and give an example (e.g. l**oo**se)

Next the tutor asks the student to listen carefully and slowly repeat some 'long vowel' words after him:

door, deer, daisy, load, receive, car, boy, crow

Ask the student: 'Did you hear any long sounds, e.g. in the word **door**?' Present the student with the written copy of these words.

Tutor and student should say the words again, leaving a pause between each word. The student is asked to underline or highlight in colour the part of the word where they hear the long vowel sound.

```
Long vowels:

door, deer, daisy, load, receive
car, boy, crow, nose
```

TRTS THE RIGHT WORDS

Get the students to point to the long vowels they have identified. (If they get it wrong do the exercise again and ask them to listen carefully).

Praise the student. Explain the long vowel (rules) patterns

e.g. /O/ can be **o-e** as in **r<u>o</u>s<u>e</u>**
or '**oa**' as in **s<u>oa</u>k, cr<u>oa</u>k**
or '**ow**' as in **cr<u>ow</u>, m<u>ow</u>, sl<u>ow</u>**

Together, begin to list as many words as you can with the **oo ee ai oa ei ar oy o-e** or **ow** vowel patterns.

The student should use colour to distinguish the long vowels and can add to the list each week/every time they come across long vowels. The list can be built up slowly and recorded in a student's personal spelling book or used, with colour and images, as a wall display:

oo	**ee**	**ai**
l<u>oo</u>se	f<u>ee</u>t	l<u>ai</u>r
moose	beet	hair
g<u>oo</u>se	s<u>ee</u>m	pair
r<u>oo</u>m	m<u>ee</u>t	
zoom		
doom		

Finally, as well as worksheets, creative activities can be given to help the student to identify, understand and use long vowels:

Exercise:
Write 4 sentences about what you did this morning using as many words with long vowels as you can. You can make it up completely!

Homophones/Confusibles/Silent letters (Ww/E3)

Homophones and confusibles (a more general, generous category covering words that are confusing or difficult) are listed in the Curriculum at E3 in the overall graphophonics scheme. For me this is slightly misleading as learners at all levels will benefit from work in this area. Students at E1 are often frustrated by confusions between **no** and **know**; **there** and **their**, whereas learners at E3 or Level 1 may point to more advanced or technical confusions: **viscous** or **vicious**, **accommodate** or **acommodate**? The difference as regards level here is the length and complexity of the words being studied rather than anything intrinsic to the topic.

Homophones are words which are pronounced/sound the same but which are spelled differently and have different meanings:

boar	bore
feat	feet
know	no
there	their

Note: It is important not to teach homophones together as this will inevitably confuse the student. Instead make a note – or better still get them to make a note – of any homophones that cause problems. Put these on separate weeks into the LOOK, COVER, WRITE, CHECK spelling programme (see Section 4). If a student encounters them in a text or needs to use both in written work encourage them to give each homophone a different colour.

Confusibles are words which are often confused for each other and often spelled incorrectly or used in the wrong context:

assess	assessed
loan	borrow
sought	bought

The best way to teach confusibles is by linking their particular sound and visual characteristics to the specific context in which they should be used. Rhymes and other mnemonic tools can be used:

TRTS THE RIGHT WORDS

<u>**Have You Any Cash?**</u>
**In life wherever you my roam, remember that
beggars always <u>borrow</u>
Lords and lenders always <u>loan</u>**

Some like **bought, sought** and taught also contain silent letter combinations (the '**gh**' here) that also commonly create difficulties in spelling. Get the student to identify and work on silent letters clusters. Regular work on and writing of these, plus an awareness of silent letter combinations is recommended.

Homonyms are a sub-type. These are words with one spelling but with several different meanings:

> **lead** (as in 'the metal')
> **lead** (as 'a dog lead')

Not all students will have problems with homophones but most, if not all, will have some problems with the more general category of confusibles or silent letters. Those few with no problems in his area can, anyway, attend group sessions and offer valuable advice to the rest of us on how they cope!

Section Summary

- As a topic for study of and work on spelling, graphophonics is very valuable.

- It should, however, only be part of a range of strategies used with students.

- Ensure that endless worksheets on long vowels or digraphs are not used and that what worksheets are used contain images and other points of interest. For a ready supply of imaginative worksheets see Elizabeth Wood's *Exercise Your Spelling* and *Strengthen Your Spelling*.

- Those tutors new to the topic should take time to acquaint themselves with the sub-topics and vocabulary: suffixes, syllables, digraphs.

- Teach homophones separately.

- Use rhyme and colour alongside writing whilst teaching this topic.

- Use activities to make sure that sub-topics such as syllables are not made dull: for example audio or video interviews could be compared by students to look at how different accents emphasise different syllables.

Section 4: OTHER STRATEGIES

Using a Range of Strategies

Arriving at the correct spelling involves a range of skills and skill combinations: reading effectively for context, fine motor co-ordination, visual recognition, phonic segmentation and recognising errors. This actually requires an amazing amount of co-ordination by the brain, the muscles and the senses. In terms of the Curriculum a number of widely scattered elements are implicated in spelling: reading ability, reading comprehension, writing skills, editing skills and knowledge/accurate recall of spelling 'rules' or patterns are all involved. This is why the Curriculum, pragmatically, emphasises that work on literacy needs to be done in an integrated, three-dimensional way. This emphasis on the three-dimensional nature of effective learning in literacy underpins much of this Section.

Section 3 looked at graphophonical strategies available to help learners spell correctly. This Section widens the net and includes a range of other, equally important strategies many of which involve a wide range of skills across the breadth of literacy. Of these the LOOK, WRITE, COVER, CHECK method is the most useful and can be extremely effective with a wide range of learners.

It is a general truth that, whatever methods and approaches are picked to improve spelling, the wider the range of strategies available the more chance of improvement by the student. Often a combination of strategies can be the most effective set of tools for learning and progression and often each individual works best with a different combination, so try them out!

This Section describes how the teacher can:

- **Carry out a spelling programme using a range of strategies**. Each strategy is summarised and briefly evaluated. Guidance is given as to which strategies are best suited to particular learning styles and to particular levels within the Curriculum. As with other sections, advice is also given on the practicalities of teaching spelling, such as the student keeping a spelling diary. Advice is also given on how to tackle the situation when a learner fails to keep to the spelling programme.
- **Record these strategies on an ILP.** Tony and Jill's ILPs are given at the end of this Section as examples of how to do this. Tony and Jill's ILPs also, I hope, make it clear how, potentially abstract elements within the Curriculum relating to spelling can work in reality and in relation to an individual's needs. This is key to the three-dimensional approach which the Curriculum advocates.

Look, Cover, Write, Check

The core of the Spelling Programme should be the LOOK, COVER, WRITE, CHECK method. As this tests the students as to whether they have correctly retained their chosen spellings and asks them to put these into sentences, it can be used to monitor and evidence progress in specific elements of the word focus *and* sentence focus levels with the Curriculum. This method will work at any level across the Standards and with students whom have quite different profiles and needs.

Use this method on the words the student has elected to learn – select no more than 10 words at a time. The method ensures that the words picked travel from the students' short-term memory into their long-term memory. Once in their long-term memory they will never forget how to spell them. Explain this to the learner.

TRTS THE RIGHT WORDS

- Get the learner to bring, or supply them with, an A5 exercise book or notepad (A4 paper will do but is easier to lose).

- Divide the page into 4 columns.

- Write the correct spelling of their chosen word in the Look column.

- Explain to the student that they need to:

LOOK
Look at this word, noting any areas of special difficulty – or anything unusual like double letter formations, words within words (**the** in **them**, **loo** in **look**, etc.), say the word at the same time. Get the student to close their eyes and try to see it in their mind. If they cannot, ask them to look at it again.

COVER
Cover the word, say it aloud.

WRITE
Write the word in column two. Say It when writing it down. Cover the word with a hand or a piece of card.

CHECK
Check that the word is correct. If it is move onto the next word and repeat the LOOK, COVER, WRITE, CHECK process. If not, copy the correct spelling near or above the original. Klein (1990) emphasises here that *'it is important to correct it by writing the whole word again not just by changing or adding letters. The experience of the whole word is important'*.

- The following day, they need to repeat the process and spell each word again in the third column.

- Two or three days later they should repeat the process, spelling the words in column four.

- After two or three more days the student is tested on the words by the tutor. The word is dictated to the student, they repeat it aloud and then write it.

- If they <u>incorrectly</u> spell a word …. then it is put into next week's list of 'words to learn'. If possible, ask the learner to find errors. Do not highlight any incorrect spellings in colour as this might reinforce them.

- If they cannot see their mistake do not allow them to struggle, give them the correct spelling and discuss their error. Make sure that they are following the process. Check, for example, that the student can see the word, letter-by-letter when they close their eyes.

- One week/five days later the words <u>spelled correctly</u> are put into context sentences: these are sentences in which the word would normally be used.

These sentences can be used as kernels for paragraphs or even whole texts. They also neatly dovetail with work at sentence focus.

T R T S THE RIGHT WORDS

Opposite is an extract from Tony's LOOK, COVER, WRITE, CHECK word list. Notice in the sample how I have put the days of the week next to each time Tony needs to run trough the method with his chosen words: this is to help him remember when he needs to work in the week.

Points To Remember with the LOOK, COVER, WRITE, CHECK method:

1. It is multi-sensory: the student is saying, visualising, seeing and writing the word: this is a great help to remembering the correct spelling.

2. It is very effective even for those with severe problems. Emphasise this to the student. It works because it makes sure that the words go into the long-term memory: once in there they are known for life.

3. It trains the learner to *"pay attention to the look of the word"* (Klein 1990, p.17). This is very useful throughout word focus but also extremely important within sentence focus when examining grammar, punctuation and sentence form.

4. It works on a 3-week cycle, with reinforcement during the first week:
   * establishing the correct spelling
   * testing, retention
   * putting the words in context sentences

5. It teaches about chunking: breaking up words into visually or phonetically memorable chunks. This is a spelling strategy in itself.

6. It places words in context and this can be used for sentence level work, as they develop knowledge of sentence forms and improve their grammar and punctuation.

7. It encourages independent learning. The method encourages the student to understand how they, as an individual, learn to spell and develop the independent learning required by L1 and L2.

8. It is structured and effective. This gives them the confidence to tackle new words encountered in their text level work and to use them in their own writing.

TEACHING THE POST-16 TO SPELL   57

Chunking

Chunking, although key to the LOOK component, of the LOOK, COVER, WRITE, CHECK methodology, is also a method within itself.

In the first session the teacher writes a correct spelling of a learner's chosen word and asks the student to look at the word carefully: 'do you see any patterns or bits to the word?' Prompt them if they are uncertain during the first session.
Discuss what they perceive. Break the word up according to this using either a coloured highlighted or by underlining the word chunks.

Double letters, syllables, word roots, prefixes and suffixes can all be identified and discussed.

In later sessions students can practise this method themselves and it can become a powerful method for analysing the makeup of words; new or familiar. Chunking, is a good vehicle for word level progression through the Curriculum:

- Ww E1.3: understanding of vowels and consonants – spot the vowels in the word chunks: **eat, lie, meat**.

- Ww E2.1: letter patterns – can you see the double letters, can you think of any other words with double letters: **call, fall, tall** – word families.

- Ww E3.3: let's identify the phonemes in these words and split them into syllables: **through, cool**

Chunking is primarily visual. This means that learners with visual strengths are probably going to find this more immediately accessible than those with phonic strengths (see Section 3). As the method is, however, excellent for underpinning phonics and words should be broken down into sounds-visual components it is also useful for learners with phonic strengths. Indeed, chunking is excellent for improving learners' graphophonic systems generally (see Section 3).

Chunking can be used at any level of the Curriculum. Support is needed at E1 and E2. At L1 and L2 learners should be tackling polysyllabic words independently, using their knowledge of roots, prefixes and suffixes.

TRTS THE RIGHT WORDS

Word-families

Learners with spelling problems often do not have any systematic comprehension of common spelling forms and conventions in English. Identifying word families is one, often enjoyable, way of tackling this problem and of getting learners to make sense of word spellings, word formation and structure.

The easiest way to begin teaching this approach is to use the sample text the learner has provided for assessment and their personal list as raw material. This also makes the lists more personalised and thereby increases the significance of the resulting lists. Extra words can be taken from sentence level and text level work as the words arise during the learners' study. Here is Tony's first list:

The 'ere' family: ***There   Here   Where?***

Student participation is important. Get them to categorise appropriate words into families, but be on hand to sensitively edit their lists. Often beginner, E1, E2 and even E3, students will put quite different words in their lists! It is also important for the tutor not to get carried away and overload the student with numerous examples.

Word families can be placed into a student's own personal spelling dictionary, used as the basis for classroom displays or even made into poetry!

They can be an excellent way to develop a student's vocabulary (how many times have teachers remarked that the student's only way of evaluating a topic/scenario/their own work/ or whatever, is limited to 'crap' or 'good'.

Words within Words

Words within words/lexical strategies are a useful way of looking at the structure and visual makeup of written language. This is a strategy that particularly appeals to learners with visual strengths and is easy to link to learning about the etymology and/or grammar of the English language.

Learners who have phonic strengths can also learn something here however, because the phonetic differences between words with the same root can be used as a basis for discussions about, roots suffixes and prefixes – this is addressing their weakness by teaching to their strength. It is important that the learner is active in identifying the pattern of words within words.

These can be grammatically orientated:

hated, hate

complained, complaining, complaint

Etymologically orientated:

Scot, Scots, Scotland, Scottish

Or visually-phonetically orientated:

rubble, rubber, rubbing

It is important that the students' attention is drawn to the fact that being able to spell the root/word-within-the word enables them to tackle a variety of words which share this, i.e. if Scot can be spelled they only need to be able to spell **land** and **ish** and add an **s** to be able to cover most word relating to this topic. Students at E1 or E2 and even E3 are often not alert to this fact and recognition can improve their motivation to tackle words they find difficult.

Furthermore the word-within-the word approach can be used to link with a range of other elements across the whole literacy Curriculum.

TRTS THE RIGHT WORDS

Spelling the root **Scot**, for example, with an upper case **S** is an essential part of sentence focus Ws/E1.2; Ws/E2.4; Ws/E3.3. Being able to scan for and recognise the capital letters of proper nouns is also an extremely useful part of text focus work : see Rt/E3.6, 7 and 8 for example. This, in turn, is linked to effective reading strategies and the student having a meaningful sight vocabulary: see Rw/E1.1; Rw/E2.1; Rt/E3.1.

Being able to group words, as with proper nouns like Scot, is also intrinsic to their grammatical knowledge: Rs/E3.2, and to their development of vocabulary; see Rw/L2.2.

Handwriting

Poorly formed letters and/or unreadable handwriting is an opportunity. Work on cursive (joined up writing) can often help students with their spelling as: it helps them focus on common letter combinations (**gh**, **th**); improves their confidence about writing; helps with motor memory – the hand remembers the correct spelling even if the student think they have forgotten. To work on handwriting,

- look, with the student, at what the problems are (badly formed letters, CAPS and lower case mixed, etc.).

- look at posture and hand position – is it right?

- try different pens and sorts of pen

- work on individual letters getting the student to form individual letter in rows on lined paper: **ggggg hhhhhhhh**

- next work on common letter formations in cursive chunks, e.g. **ght, sl, fi**

- work on writing whole words cursively,

and finally:

- ask the student to write a whole line/paragraph using cursive writing.

Experimental Strategies

Experimental strategies are a range of approaches that are more unusual. What is crucial is that whatever works for the learner, however unusual or even strange, is used to help them spell and tackle writing their chosen words. Pictures, mental associations, rhymes and physically modelling or tracing words can all be used – whatever works for the learner, try it! Their involvement is crucial: get them to draw, laugh at or be amazed by your drawings; create rhymes together; put smells or tastes to words; create fictional words and imagine their spelling or use. See Section 5 for an example of an experimental strategy in a teaching session:

- **Pictograms**
  e.g.

  look **look**

- **Mnemonic phrases**

  ant

  "There is an ant in my restaurant, pants, plants"

- **Rhymes**
  *"You don't have **fun** at a **funeral**"*

- **Fonts**
  Cut out newspaper words and arrange or explore the fonts on a computer with Word. What effects do different types of letter shapes (fonts) have on how the same word looks and how it feels? Try writing a simple headline in **Comic Sans** and then do so in **Times New Roman**.

- **Plastic or Foam letters**
  Use plastic or foam letters with vowels coloured red. These can be used to show letter patterns and crucially encourage active learning, as they are moveable. Try placing out common patterns, suffixes or prefixes and getting the learner to create a word.

TRTS THE RIGHT WORDS

- **Tracing (Fernald method)**
  Use a coloured pen to write words on card. The student traces with the forefinger of their writing hand ('writing finger). This can be used with the LOOK, COVER, WRITE, CHECK method to reinforce their (motor) memory of the shape of letters.

Experimental strategies are more normally used at Entry Level within the Curriculum or with students whom have more severe spelling difficulties. In this sense experimental methods seek to overcome major barriers to progression. See dealing with problems: what to do if no progress made, at the end of this section. They can also, however, be used when a more advanced learner (E1, E2) has a sudden, unexpected block with more technical or complex words.

Dictionaries

I am using this is a wide context. Dictionary use is specified within the Curriculum: 'reference material' to obtain the meaning of unfamiliar words is an element at Rw/L1.2 and at Rw/L2.2. Use of a dictionary is also specified in the descriptor at Ww/E3.1.

While use of a good basic dictionary is essential to spelling, it is however often the case that learners who are less advanced or who have more severe spelling problems cannot use a traditional dictionary: they often do not know what the initial letters of words are and so cannot even look for the correct spelling! To avoid this frustration introduce a wider concept of dictionary:

A personal spelling dictionary

This is a dictionary that they create, writing down the correct spellings of key words they have learned or are comfortable with spelling. Notebooks or even an address book, alphabetically pre-organised are ideal. The LOOK, COVER, WRITE, CHECK method can form the basis of this, at least initially. Work on the alphabet at E1 can be plugged into their alphabetical organisation of a plain notebook.

Use a visual dictionary

Visual dictionaries make the word far less abstract and therefore make it easier to tackle. Visual dictionaries are very useful when working with ESOL (English for Speakers of Other Languages) learners or those at E1, E2. They may not be appropriate for learners at higher levels – or those whom are particularly sensitive about their level of literacy.

Try using an ACE phonetic dictionary

ACE dictionaries work on sound and thereby overcome the problem of how to find a word when unsure of its initial letters. As long as the student can say it and understand the very basics of phonics they can use an ACE dictionary.

The tutor should be familiar with its use because the learner needs their initial assistance as regards the ACE system for finding words. When the student is confident they can consult it as needed. Those for whom dictionaries have often been inaccessible often value this independence.

Tasks and assignments can be constructed around dictionary use, fulfilling the objectives set out in word focus element descriptors. At E1 and E2 these can be centered on creating a personal dictionary with 'familiar key words' (Ww/E2.1).

An Assignment Example

On the next page is an assignment that Tony, our sample learner was set after 12 weeks on the spelling programme and having set up a personal dictionary. The tutor made sure that Tony understood what was expected before he started work and verbally reinforced points. Curriculum references have been put in to point out how the assignment can meet Curriculum standards; they do not need to be included in what is actually given to the student!

At E2, a learner can be introduced to a basic, visually supported dictionary and to an ACE dictionary. This lays the foundation for progression onto L1 and L2.

TRTS THE RIGHT WORDS

Phonics: Using a Tape Recorder

See Section 3 for a full explanation of how attention to phonics can develop and enhance spelling.

It is useful for phonically orientated learners to use a tape recorder when checking their spelling. This can even help those who do not have phonic strengths, as it is a multi-sensory strategy.

- After having written either a context sentence in the LOOK, COVER, WRITE, CHECK method or completed a short piece of free writing, the learner reads the piece aloud and records it onto a tape-recorder. Often mistakes will be picked up by this alone: they did not write what they meant: have used the wrong words and spelled this word incorrectly.

- Once recorded the learner listens to their reading and follows their written version. Errors in spelling and other problems will usually be identified.

This is an excellent method for sentence focus, and text focus work too, because it focuses on 'meaning' when composing and reading text. Checking for appropriate meaning, both in what they have personally written and in reading comprehension, is often lacking with beginner learners. This task develops these skills, using the ear as a key editing and analysis tool, as well as the eye.

Editing

As the above indicates, accurate spelling relies on accurate, careful reading: they are interdependent. Encourage the student to use a staged reading of their writing:

- In the FIRST stage check for MEANING. Is this what they want to say to the reader? Do sentences make sense?

- In the SECOND stage check for PUNCTUATION. Where are the full stops, commas and capital letters?

- In the THIRD stage check SPELLING. Read carefully, look at the words. Are their any words that look wrong? Do they need to check any words using their personal dictionary (E1 and E2) ACE dictionary (E2 and above) or general dictionary? Whom can they ask for advice on whether the word is the right one in this context?

Finally, the learner should re-read the whole text normally. See Section 2 for integration of word focus and sentence level work within the Curriculum and Section 5 for further examples of this in practice.

The Student Often Knows Best

An individual's own approaches are often very important because we often know what works for ourselves. Ask the student what strategies they use to remember how to spell words. With tutor direction and elaboration this builds up awareness of their own strategies and of how these can be developed by the approaches outlined in this section. This is key to developing independent learning. Identifying, sharing and trying students' own approaches is an excellent basis for a group session. Section 5 gives further detail of this teaching strategy and offers a lesson based around it.

TRTS THE RIGHT WORDS

Tony and Jill's ILPs

We have followed Tony and Jill through the process of assessment and the selection of suitable strategies based on their specific needs. On the following pages are their final formal ILPs.

More detail has been added than is usually required and to make things clearer the relevant references to Curriculum elements have been added.

INDIVIDUAL LEARNING PLAN

Student Name: **JILL DAVIES**
Course: BTEC Drama
Course Tutor: S. Mckenzie

AIMS

- Work on spelling to fit in with work on grammar and sentence-use.

- Jill to stick to Spelling Programme, especially *Look, Cover, Write, Check.*

- Increase vocabulary: spell new words confidently, link work on spelling with reading (Brecht, Alan Bennett, Stanislavski) and course writing: BTEC Assignments.

- Improve own editing/proofreading skills via regular use of a dictionary and thesaurus (not Roget's – alphabetically organised thesaurus instead).

- Use of the college library for research and let me see your first drafts of assignments.

- Improve confidence with technical performance words: Jill to set up technical dictionary.

- Increase own study skills: Jill is to identify problem words for Spelling Programme.

- Know and apply a range of methods to help with spelling: work on vowels and phonics.

- Know common spelling patterns in English, recognise and tackle irregular spellings.

TRTS THE RIGHT WORDS

INDIVIDUAL LEARNING PLAN
OBJECTIVES
(how the aims will be met in specific, time-bound, measurable steps)

Student Name: **JILL DAVIES**
Day/time: Thurs 9.30 am – 12.00
Teaching Style: 1:1, Group every 2nd week
Tutor: D. Armstrong

Spelling work to reinforce work on grammar and sentence use, e.g. dictation sentences in *Look, Cover, Write, Check* should be complex sentences. Work on spelling grammar terms: 'conjunctions', 'adjectives', 'vocabulary' and 'grammatical'. (Ws/L1.1)

Once every 2 weeks. Jill to rewrite sections of course reading in her own words, but keeping any technical language intact and identifying main points. After proof-reading, punctuation, grammar and spelling should all be correct. (Rt/L1.3) (Ws/L1.1, 2.3) (Wt/L2.7)

Jill to note down and clarify meaning of any technical language: (Rt/L1.4) using appropriate aids: dictionary, Drama Encyclopaedia. She should be able to spell key org. features, e.g. 'glossary' 'abbreviations' and 'introduction'. (Rt/L1.4, Rw/L1)

These spellings should go into a personal dictionary (Rw/E3.1, 3, 4 and 5)

Work on vowels, vowel clusters and syllables (Ww/E2.2 and Ww/E3.2)

After guidance she must show she can select the right mode of address, type of content, level of detail and persuasive language in 'Evaluate' assignments (Wt/L2.1, 2, 3, 4, 5 and 6) being able to spell key words: 'persuade', 'argument' 'evaluate' 'compare', 'contrast' and 'assess'.

Jill is to start and regularly fill in a list of these assignment words in her personal dictionary. They should be spelled correctly.

Pick out and spell collective nouns: 'actors'; 'people'; 'society'; 'audience'. (Rw/L1: 1,2, 3)

Worksheets, advice and practice on using spelling rules. Work on word-families: 'perform, performance, performing, performer and performed'.

Signed Student: Jill Davies
Signed Tutor: D. Armstrong
Date: 20/09/03

INDIVIDUAL LEARNING PLAN

Student Name: **TONY SMITH**
Course: GNVQ Mech.
Tutor: B. Reiss

AIMS

- Improve handwriting (legibility, letter formation).

- Hand in 1 short piece of writing every 2 weeks which has been planned and proofread.

- Tony to stick to Spelling Programme: especially *Look, Cover, Write, Check.*

- Increase vocabulary: spell new words confidently, link work on spelling with reading and course writing.

- Improve own editing/proofreading skills. Regular use of a dictionary.

- Use of the college library for magazines/internet materials to be used in free writing.

- Improve confidence with trade/garage paperwork i.e. parts requisition forms.

- Increase own study skills: Tony is to identify problems words for Spelling Programme, set-up and maintain a personal spelling dictionary.

- Know and apply a range of methods to help with spelling.

- Know common spelling patterns in English, recognise and tackle irregular spellings.

TRTS THE RIGHT WORDS

INDIVIDUAL LEARNING PLAN
OBJECTIVES
(how the aims will be met in specific, time-bound, measurable steps)

Student Name: **TONY SMITH**
Day/time: Wed and Thurs 1-3pm
Teaching Style: 1:1, Group every 2nd week
Tutor: D. Armstrong

Handwriting: work on double letters: letter size and formation. Tony to try a range of pens, look at posture, practise letter strings (mmmm, rrrrrrrr) after picking out his problem letters. (Ww/ E2.3)

Tony to write about his team's matches/new car models every week. He should read car 'Car Monthly' or newspapers on Saturday to help him do this. He can pick other topics but still must read-up on them. He can use the internet. (Wt/E3.1, 2, 3 and 4). The written piece should be planned, proofread and written in sentences. (Ws/E3.1). He can use a spellchecker.

He will be shown how to plan and do a staged proof-reading (I = Tony). He will practise this on his own writing. (Wt/E3.4)

He needs to learn 3 new words every week and write them, with meanings, in his personal spelling dictionary. He needs to buy and use a general dictionary. (Rw/E3.1, 2, 3 and 4; Ww E2.1 and 2)

Stick to the spelling programme: 8 words each week. Three words have to be from something Tony has read. (Rt/E3, Ww/L1.1)

Work on Syllables (2, 3 then 3+); work on plurals. (Ww/E2.2)

Worksheets, advice and practice on using spelling rules.

Work on word-families: 'drive', 'drove', 'driven'.

Work on irregular spellings (not everything is spelled as it sounds!): 'ch' saying /k/ (mechanic) (Ww E3.1). Work on silent sounds: 'receipt' and common formations i.e. 'write', 'wrist'. (Rw/E3.5)

Signed Student: Tony Smith
Signed Tutor: David Armstrong
Date: 20/09/03

TEACHING THE POST-16 TO SPELL   71

What to do when nothing seems to be working

Regular assessment and review is essential to developing literacy and will alert teacher and learner to any lack of progress in spelling specifically. ILPs need to be reviewed every 6 weeks but it is also good practice to have, or aim for, a semi-formal review every two weeks.

The spelling programme outlined in this section, through weekly testing in the LOOK, COVER, WRITE, CHECK method, has monitoring of progress built into it. This is the crux of progress in spelling - ensure that the student sticks to it. Be firm about this and underline how sticking to LOOK, COVER, WRITE, CHECK, is certain to improve their spelling, no matter what their past problems in this area.

Is flagging motivation an issue? Occasionally students will flounder due to a lapse in motivation. If this is the case re-remind them of the objectives set out in their learning plan and underline their recent progress.

One of the greatest problems that students who are improving their literacy face, is overcoming the demotivating legacy of what they may see as educational failure and of why they percieve themselves as not as successful as others in this area. Interest in the subject matter is a key tool that can be used to combat this potential barrier partly because it leads them to just engage with study rather than worry about percieved failings or poor outcomes.

Motivation is also a key element if the student is to adopt the kind of focus and overall mental attitude necessary for progress. Interest, focus, action and evaluation (often in this order) are all needed within the kind of efficent study necessary for developing spelling and, indeed, any aspect of literacy. The medium-term goal is to encourage the student to develop a positive, efficient and confident study practice. The long term-goal is to see them be able to have the educational tools and self-discipline to develop independently.

Being explicit and open about why you are asking them to work in a particular

TRTS THE RIGHT WORDS

way is very useful here - particularly with those who have had a previously negative experience of education: "I am asking you to try this because...This will help, trust me, because...Spelling and reading are related, believe me, this is because..."

Section Summary

- Ensure a range of strategies are used, including ones the learner already uses with success. The LOOK, COVER, WRITE, CHECK should be the central approach of the spelling programme but try other methods: whatever works for your learner is a tool to be exploited.

- Monitor and evaluate their progress. Are they sticking to the LOOK, COVER, WRITE, CHECK method? What progress is being made in the words they initially identified? Are they aware that visual as well as phonic strategies are required to spell well? Is their interest waning?

- Record problems, progress and achievement on the ILP. Ticking off Curriculum reference descriptors is a practical way of recording progress.

- Be positive and help your learner be positive about improving their spelling.

Section 5: SOME SAMPLE SESSIONS

Introduction

To make what has gone before this point less abstract and also to provide a welcome break from a focus on 1:1 work here are four group sessions.

Wherever possible, guidance is given on how each session can fit into other work within the Curriculum. This integration is important not only because the Curriculum underlines the need for an integrated approach but also because the learner needs to perceive the relationships between good spelling, a strong vocabulary and efficient reading.

Elements from speaking and listening parts of the curriculum have not been included, but I hope that student compliance with what the sessions ask of them will meet many of the criteria at Entry Level 2 and above.

Session 1: Graphophonic

Aims

1. To introduce the concepts of 'confusible' words (Ww/E3.1) and reinforce the notion that sound (phonemes) and look (grapheme) are in a relationship: (Ww/E1.1 and 3; Ww/E2.2, Rw/E1.1 and 2; Rw/E2.2).

2. To reinforce previous work on key graphophonic elements: digraphs, blends, consonants, vowels and silent letters (Rw/E2.2).

3. To allow the learners to identify these key elements themselves and be aware of their own strengths and weaknesses (a skill across all the elements).

TRTS THE RIGHT WORDS

4. To encourage each learner to learn from each other and the group experience while also working at their own pace and at their own level (differentiation).

Objectives
Via the group setting and a selection of whole group and pair work the above aims will be met.

Duration
Approximately one-and-a half-hours but can be extended depending upon the needs of those within the group.

Resources
Flipchart or white-board, coloured markers: a 'prompt' list of words with silent letters and that are often confused (confusibles).

Method and Content

- Introduce the topic keeping technical description (i.e. homophones, homonyms) to a minimum.

- Split the class into small groups or pairs and direct the students to identify any/several words which they find 'confusing' - If necessary prompt.

- Bring the groups together and compile a list on the wipeboard or flipchart from their responses. Discuss these problems words

- Ask: *'Is there anything that stands out about how any of these words sound or look?'*

- Lead the discussion taking contributions from individuals, link with any prior work on phonemic-visual components such as digraphs, blends, consonants, vowels or common endings.

- Explain that for homophones, confusibles and silent letters the best way to learn is through the individual spelling programme which everybody present is going to start next session (this is a good introduction).

- Explain that the best way to learn homophones is by learning them one at a time and by writing the word in context, often, otherwise it is easy to get confused. Give an example.

> Bilbo the magician did a <u>feat</u> of magic.
> 'Climbing that mountain was a <u>feat</u>' said the climber.

- Explain to the group: **feat** = something impressive, something that most people can't do.

- Pose the question: *'if you wanted to impress somebody special/the world in general what would you do?'*

- After 5 minutes go around the group one-by-one and ask for answers.

- Afterwards, get each individual to write out their 'feat'.

- Pass around coloured highlighters get each individual to highlight the 'a' in feat (if working with a confident group get them to explain why the 'a' in their 'fe<u>a</u>t' stands for something <u>a</u>mazing).

Return to the homophones/confusibles highlighted by learners
Open up the session: *'how does anybody present here cope with these words, can you give us any tips?*

- Discuss and analyse students' strategies
- Can they be applied to other homophones/confusibles?
- How useful are they?

By the end of the session ensure that learners have identified all or several of the words that they find problematic. These need to be placed into a student's Individual Spelling Programme. This session can also be used to help the learner produce a personal dictionary. This is a lined A5 exercise book/notebook where the learner alphabetically lists 'problem' words and writes their meaning next to the word. Creating a personal dictionary is an excellent activity for those improving their spelling. It is both an active and meaningful way for learners to tackle 'difficult' words. See Section 4 for further advice.

Work on graphophonics can be extended and enriched by work on visualisation, accent, rhyme and rhythm, see the session on rhyme in this section and also Section 4 for examples.

TRTS THE RIGHT WORDS

Session 2: Top 10

Aims

1. To introduce the concepts of setting targets for improving spelling and to identify a list of key words which the learner can work on in their individual Spelling Programme and satisfy key elements within the Adult Literacy Core Curriculum: Ww/E2.1 'spell correctly the majority of personal details and familiar common words'. Also covered is: Ww/E3.1 and 2: 'spell correctly common words and relevant key words for work and special interest'. Other elements touched upon: Rw/E3.1, 2 and 5, also contributing toward more specialist vocabulary in Rw/L2.1.

2. To allow the learners to identify their personal list of difficult words and be aware of own strengths and weaknesses.

3. To introduce the methodology of chunking.

4. To link up with other elements within the Adult Literacy Core Curriculum, e.g. reading - from which 'difficult' words can be selected or taken from a social sight vocabulary within Rw/E1 for example.

5. To encourage each learner to learn from each other and the group experience while also working at their own pace and at their own level (differentiation).

Objectives

Via the group setting and a selection of whole group and small group work the above aims will be met.

Duration

Approximately one-and-a half-hours but can be extended depending upon the needs of those within the group.

Resources

Flipchart or white-board, flipchart markers and flipchart paper.

Method and Content

Introduce lesson and concept of 'Top Ten' using pop music analogy.

Ask group to split into small groups or pairs. Ensure each group has a basic dictionary, a selection of flipchart pens and 2 sheets of flipchart paper. Set them the task: To identify a top 10 of words which are difficult to spell, number 1 being the most difficult. They have half an hour, if necessary, to do this. Explain they can rank and write their findings on the flipchart paper and that they can use the dictionary to help them spell or ask each other for help. Emphasise that wrong spellings or bad handwriting, however, will not be penalised: these are the words from hell after all!

Visit each group during the time, overseeing and assisting. Be supportive to learners with poor handwriting. Those who finish early can assist others or can discuss their top 10.

After half-an-hour bring the group together. Collect their flipchart sheets. Discuss each selection as a whole group and get the writers to say why they selected each word. The strategy of chunking can be demonstrated to the whole group here by the teacher using the flipchart, several words from the students' top 10 and a selection of coloured markers. If necessary have a break now.

Top 10: Spellings from Hell

1. accommodate
2. their
3. dyslexia
4. psychology
5. recommend
6. stationary
7. attendance
8. receipt
9. college
10. separate

Ask the original groups to reform. Redistribute the sheets to their respective owners. Ask each to identify which words out of their top 10 do they need to learn for everyday life, work or study.

TRTS THE RIGHT WORDS

Reconvene the whole group. Discuss each group's new findings. Emphasise to the whole group that these words should be their priority and that selecting a priority list of problem words is very important when improving spelling. Explain that this needs to be done regularly and that these words can be taken from their reading, study, everyday life or work. Ask each individual to now compile their individual top 10 of words that they need or desire to learn how to spell.

Conclude the session by underlining how identifying key words whose spelling can be improved is also key to success and that the final top 10 that each individual has compiled is the basis for their progress in spelling.

Session 3: Orlop

Aims
- To identify skills and strategies used to approach, decode and learn new and unfamiliar words. This is covered by all the elements: Rw/E2.3, 4 and 5, Rw/E3.3 and 5, Rw/L1.2 and 3.

- To share the above strategies in a supportive setting.

- To link in with other sessions within the Curriculum, e.g. 'know and use the term adjective' Ws/E2.2 and sessions on using the dictionary covered by Rw/L1.1 and Rw/L2.2.

- To introduce students to a tool for expanding vocabulary – a personal dictionary – and show them how to use this tool.

Objectives
Via the group setting and whole group discussions plus the aims set for each individual within the group, the above will be met

Duration
Approximately one-and-a half-hours but can be extended depending upon the needs of those within the group

Resources
Flipchart or white-board, and a selection of notebooks which can be given

out as personal dictionaries. A selection of easy-to-use dictionaries are also required.

Method and Content

- Introduce the session outlining its content.
- Begin with a question: how do we learn new words?
- Write **orlop** (or another short unknown word) on the flipchart/ whiteboard.
- Invite questions with the prompt: Is it an animal, object, place, illness, food or something else?
- Host a discussion. Invite learners to offer an unusual word that they have heard or read recently: this is a good place to link in with text-focus work.
- Introduce the information that the tutor has never found out what **orlop** means so, the class will have to agree a meaning for the word!

Lead discussion suggesting useful strategies for correct spelling use of new words. Take contributions from learners about how they deal with and internalise words with which they are unfamiliar. Introduce the concepts of:

- **reading**: we need to be able to read **orlop** to be able to spell it. Let's all agree how we say it.
- **reference**: we might go to a dictionary to look up **orlop** – what kind of a dictionary would we use? Does everybody have access to a dictionary here?
- **word 'families' and patterns**: **orlop, orloping, orlopery** and **orlopated**?
- **context**: where might **orlop** be used? We need to practise writing and saying orlop in the right context to get the correct context.
- **adjectives** – is **orlop** an adjective? What are adjectives?

The tutor should explain that a personal dictionary is a good tool through which to learn to spell new words. Explain that this is a notebook used by the student where they record new words, placing a definition next to

TRTS THE RIGHT WORDS

each entry. The meaning can be in the students' own language, as long as they can read and understand it – or taken from a dictionary which they can understand. The tutor can pass around a selection of accessible dictionaries at this point.

Explain that the best words to start with are those which they find interesting or which they need to learn for everyday life, work or study. The tutor can give examples on the whiteboard.

Finally, summarise the session and set the group a goal. Each learner is to:

> Identify 3 new words each week and either on their own, or with help from the tutor. They are to use them either in written work or place them into their individual spelling programme or alternatively into their own personal dictionary. This goal can also be recorded on their ILP.

The students' aim should be to:

- say them using the correct pronunciation
- spell them correctly
- know their place of use and what they mean

Session 4: Rhyme Challenge

Aims
To promote graphophonic skills, allow learners to develop these skills and to assist an awareness of spelling patterns. This session can meet elements across the word focus part of the curriculum. It also meets some criteria on text focus sections of the curriculum: Rw /E2.3 'use phonic and graphic knowledge to decode words' for example; and can be linked to work on punctuation and capitalisation: Rs/E3.3. Discussing then planning, writing and finally editing simple rhymes covers almost every skill.

Objectives
The above aims are met via construction of simple rhymes and nonsense poems.

Duration

Approximately three hours, with a 15-minute break, but can be extended or decreased depending upon the needs of those within the group

Resources

Flipchart or a white-board, flipchart markers and flipchart paper, plus a selection of newspapers/magazines and several pairs of scissors. Also, several poems taken from *The Book of Nonsense and Nonsense Songs* by Edward Lear – available in Penguin Popular Poetry. A prize can be awarded at the tutors' discretion.

Method and Content

Introduce the idea of rhyme (as opposed to poetry – do not mention poetry as this may have negative connotations for some learners). Throw open the question to the group: what is rhyme? What do words that rhyme have in common?

From the discussion select or introduce a selection of words, steering the discussion about them in terms of:

- how they look: common visual patterns
- how they sound: common sound patterns

To add interest, at this point ask a selected member of the group to say the consonants **w, m, b** and **p**. Ask them which part of their mouth did they use? (they will use their lips)

Ask another member of the group to say the consonants **n, s, l, t, r, th** and **d**. (they will use their tongue).

The tutor should emphasise that if words are looked at closely – in terms of how they sound or how they look - patterns soon appear and that looking for these patterns will help with spelling.

Split the whole group into small groups issuing each with a selection of newspapers and magazines. Their challenge is to find as many words as

TRTS THE RIGHT WORDS

they can which rhyme and to cut out these words using the scissors: they have 20 minutes – go!

Progress can be monitored by the tutor: are they picking words which really rhyme? After 20 minutes have elapsed, provide a break.

When reconvened, ask each group to place rhyming words next to each other or in groups/rows, ask them to provide a count of the words they have identified. Ask each group for a tally of words and get a representative from each to discuss any which were amusing, or significant. The winner is praised (or can be awarded a prize at the tutors' discretion).

Handout a suitable poem from *The Book of Nonsense and Nonsense Songs* by Edward Lear – ensure every individual has a copy. Read the poem aloud. Ask them to quickly underline all the words which rhyme.

Invite comments about structure and content, draw attention to pairs of rhyming lines (couplets) underlining how only the last words rhyme.

Split into small groups: ask each group to create a small rhyme emphasising that it does not have to actually make sense but needs to use real words (confident individuals can create rhymes on their own if they wish). The tutor can offer prompts if necessary:

> Death,
> Rock and Roll,
> A Sunny Day,
> Christmas,
> A Recent Pop Idol,
> Football Forever

Every individual in the groups needs to write out their own copy of the collective poem (rather than leave the writing to just one group scribe) but suggest that they try to work it out verbally before committing to paper. They can even take it in turns to write lines. They have 30 minutes. Assist individuals or groups as necessary.

Reconvene the session and invite each group to read their poem or if they prefer, the tutor can read them.

- Congratulate the whole group – what poetry!

Remind the group that rhyme is about patterns and that recognising common spelling patterns can really improve spelling.

After typing up or re-writing the resulting poems can be mounted onto card and used to decorate the rooms where sessions are held: these are active reminders of the session content. Images and colours can be used to add texture.

TRTS **THE RIGHT WORDS**

CONCLUSION
Something To Take-away For Life

The Introduction set out why spelling was an important issue to tackle for learners. As was pointed out earlier in this publication, good spelling has positive knock-on effects across a person's overall literacy. It also has wider ripple effects across an individual's overall education, motivation to succeed and can even affect a student's behaviour. The feeling that a problem is slowly lifting through their efforts and that new skills are being developed can have a catalytic impact upon literacy and upon wider learning. It often gives the student an enormous feeling of progress and achievement.

Long-term benefits of improved spelling include:

- Increased motivation to go out and tackle new or unfamiliar words

- The confidence and ability to edit writing with minimal support from others.

- Improved skills in predicting spelling patterns when approaching new words.

- Improved confidence in writing generally.

- An increase in both the quantity and quality of writing.

- An improved sense of how they feel about themselves and their learning generally.

- A feeling that a persistent, nagging problem has been addressed.

- More confidence in personal reading skills and the student reading more frequently.

Ideally, at the end of your tuition on spelling these are the feelings, attitudes and skills that the learner should carry for life.

TRTS THE RIGHT WORDS

CURRICULUM INDEX

Book page numbers for curriculum references